WHAT OTHERS ARE SA

I have always maintained that those who clarify their value the best win. And David is easily one of the best sales enablement executives to help your company do just that. He puts customers and their needs at the center of every story, and then helps you build and crystallize your unique value proposition around those needs, versus just your feature set. This makes all the difference in B2B selling, and as a result, we were able to double our revenues at the companies I have worked with over the past several years.

— Joanne Moretti,
CRO (Chief Revenue Officer), Fictiv

Essential to high performance sales and customer success is the ability for customer-facing professionals to understand, articulate, and deliver outcome-oriented conversations with prospects and customers. While most sales professionals fancy themselves as value-oriented solution sellers, the sad truth from the perspective of buyers is that 80% or more of sales conversations are product/feature/function in nature. It's not surprising that the vast majority of buyers prefer not to deal with sales reps at all. It's not just the fault of sales reps, though; organizations do a poor job of enablement.

David Kurkjian demonstrates the ability to assimilate the beneficial constructs for a go-to-market strategy and codify those constructs into a repeatable "cookbook" for reps to follow. The result of making reps better in front of prospects and customers is worth it's weight in quota-achieving gold. I highly recommend the MasterMessaging approach, and *6X – Convert More Prospects to Customers* articulates these invaluable principles masterfully.

— Jim Berryhill,
Founder, DecisionLink

David has a unique capability to deeply understand human behavior and motivations, and how to translate these insights into actions that will allow sales teams to be more effective, strategic, and impactful. Any sales professional should read this book!

- Uri Levy,
SVP (Senior Vice President),
Worldwide Sales XM Cyber

I stopped reading traditional business books after I met David. I realized there is a whole different level of knowledge to understand and leverage in order to get better results. The world is better off now that this information is in his book, and I highly recommend every business leader reading and applying it.

— Jason Pace,
COO (Chief Operating Officer),
Diversified Metal Fabricators

6X
CONVERT MORE PROSPECTS TO CUSTOMERS

A ROAD MAP FOR EARLY-STAGE SALES CONVERSATIONS

DAVID KURKJIAN

CONTENTS

INTRODUCTION

Coffee. Jeans. TV stations. What do these three things have in common?

If you were to travel back in time to the 1960s, you would find limited choices in all three categories.

Coffee: You'd be drinking Folgers or Maxwell House.

Jeans: After Marlon Brando and James Dean popularized them, you were looking at buying either Levis or Wranglers.

TV stations: CBS, NBC, ABC, and PBS. That's it. At midnight they would play the national anthem and sign off. No choices after that.

Fast forward to today, and you have overwhelming options in each of these three categories. Coffee shops specialize in coffees from all over the world. Jeans, you can choose from designer jeans to knock offs on Amazon or other retail outlets. TV stations, across all the different options, easily in the hundreds.

The reality is we live in a commoditized world. Not just in what we as consumers can buy but also in the business world. Every problem that business professionals face, they have numerous choices in how to solve them.

Now add the internet to the equation of choice. Buyers have a wealth of information to help them understand the best ways to solve their problems. Back before the internet was around, buyers relied on the sellers to educate them about possible solutions that their products and services could provide. This created a dynamic where the salesperson had to be an expert in their field to succeed. In this scenario, product expertise was the most important skill.

Every problem that business professionals face, they have numerous choices in how to solve them.

This showed up in a recent conversation with my father.

He was in industrial sales throughout his career selling electric motors, variable speed drives, and other equipment used in manufacturing. He earned his bachelor's degree in industrial engineering at Michigan State. I asked him what one thing contributed to his success in sales. He answered his engineering license. When I asked him why, he replied, "the technical expertise along with the credibility the license provided in talking with my prospects." In other words, his product and technical knowledge helped differentiate him from his competitors. But a lot has changed since he stepped into retirement at the turn of the century.

Recent studies show that in today's world, buyers do their research online and engage sales professionals much later in the buyer's journey. Here's a quote from a recent Gartner study: "Sellers have little opportunity to influence customer decisions. The ready availability of quality information through digital channels has made it far easier for buyers to gather information independently, meaning sellers have less access and fewer opportunities to influence customer decisions. In fact, Gartner research finds that when B2B buyers are considering a purchase, they spend only 17% of that time meeting with potential suppliers. When buyers are comparing multiple suppliers, the amount of time spent with any one sales rep may be only 5% or 6%" (Gartner, n.d.).

What this means is you have a very small window of opportunity to differentiate yourself from the competition and clearly communicate the unique value represented in your product or service.

What this means is you have a very small window of opportunity to differentiate yourself from the competition and clearly communicate the unique value represented in your product or service. Since the buyer is mostly up to speed on the different options they can choose from, the salesperson's skill shifts from product knowledge to communication. Specifically, how you talk about your product or service in your selling conversations.

With these challenges as a backdrop:

- What if you could more easily engage your prospects?
- What if you could elevate the perceived value of your product or service?
- Finally, what if you could move more prospects through the early stages of the buyer's journey?

You can with the principles and techniques you'll learn in this book.

You'll better understand the buying mind and how it perceives value. You'll know how to communicate with prospects and customers in a way that is simple, clear, and easy to remember. Then you'll see how to build high value conversations with a simple sales conversation road map. Toward the end, you'll get to bonuses, an example discovery call, and a chapter on negotiations.

As an industrial engineer by education (yes, I followed the same path as my father), I've always been intrigued by how things work. During the process of starting MasterMessaging, my sales consultancy company, I brought that intrigue and focus on behavioral psychology and how human beings make decisions. The reasoning behind this is that understanding the decision-making process would help me identify specific principles and techniques for sales professionals that would make it easier to communicate their unique value to prospects and customers. Techniques that would not only help differentiate the product but also differentiate the buyer's experience.

I took what I learned about the psychology of decision and combined it with thirty years of selling experience. Starting with my early career at BellSouth, then building sales teams with CareerBuilder in the 90s, and perfecting the art of communicating value with several startups in the 2000s.

What you'll find in the chapters ahead are:

- A basic understanding of the science of decision;
- A SUCCESS formula for speaking the language of decision;
- A road map for building high-value conversations;
- Techniques specific to objection handling, white boarding, and negotiations.

All this to make it simpler for you to clearly communicate your value and make it easier for the buyer to say "Yes!"

You'll read later in the book about the purpose of "6X" (from the title). One of the first sales teams I taught this information to was at a software company. After a single financial quarter, they increased their first call conversion rate from 8% to 47% using the newly-learned methods that are contained within this book. They didn't hire or fire anyone; they didn't need any drastic changes in services or products. Instead, all they needed was the right perspective and mindset to start converting prospects to customers, maximizing their value, and increasing their potential customer base by a factor of six.

Are you ready for that kind of success?

CHAPTER 1

DEVELOP A WINNING MINDSET

*"Great salespeople are relationship
builders who provide value and
help their customers win."*
— Jeffrey Gitomer

This statement by Jeffrey Gitomer succinctly describes a winning mindset in this field.

Consider this common scenario:

A sales leader is meeting with a salesperson and reviewing why they lost a deal. The typical answers are: We were too expensive, the competition is better, marketing collateral is no good, or any number of things that have nothing to do with the salesperson.

What the salesperson is missing in this scenario is that success in selling is all about what a salesperson brings to the relationship with a prospect or customer. It's too easy to put the blame of lack of success on marketing, sales leadership, the product, or anything that you don't have control over.

The truth is that the salesperson has control over several skills. Communication, product knowledge, negotiation, presentation, and insightful questions are just the beginning. However, the most important asset is a winning mindset.

In order to develop a winning mindset as a salesperson, let's first look at the definition of a salesperson (Cambridge Dictionary n.d.).

salesperson (noun)

: *a person whose job is to sell things*

At first glance, the definition of a salesperson looks pretty straight-forward: A person who sells things. But that's where the simplicity ends.

We've all experienced being on the receiving end of a sales conversation. Based on some of these experiences, it's easy to understand why the sales profession has gotten such a bad rap. As a matter of fact, if you look at the Gallup poll on trustworthiness for different professions, the sales profession typically falls toward the very bottom ("Honesty" n.d.). Why is that?

Consider this example of a sales conversation with a roofing company. Your home needs a new roof, so you reach out to several contractors and pick three and set up appointments.

The first company that you meet with is number one in your city, and their price reflects it. Two gentlemen show up at your door, and you welcome them into your living room. You proceed to sit there and listen to a two-hour monologue of why they are the best roofing company in the city. During that time, you speak for no more than five to ten minutes. There were no questions for you, and no focus on what's important or what you might be interested in. They delivered a lot of content on their technology, their process, their success, their reputation, and a long dissertation on how they go about installing a roof.

To make matters worse, at the end of the conversation, they offer a small discount if you are willing to sign a contract to move forward before they leave your house. You've already made up your mind before this awkward close that there was no way you'd be doing business with them. Why?

The answer is obvious: You put this under the category of a Salesperson Behaving Badly. There are a number of behaviors by a salesperson that fall under this category.

Number 1: Sharing way too much information.

As a salesperson, you're expected to be passionate about the product or service that you represent, but sometimes that passion can get in your way. There is a biological reason behind this behavior.

You'll read several ways behavioral psychology comes into play in sales throughout this book. One of these aspects of behavior shows up when you meet somebody for the very first time.

When you meet someone for the first time, you are most comfortable when you're talking about something you're passionate or knowledgeable about. The science behind this is a well-known hormone called dopamine. When you're speaking about something you're passionate or knowledgeable about, dopamine drips on your brain to make you feel good. The better you feel, the more you talk. This can lead to a feature and benefit dump in an early conversation with a prospect. In a volume of information, it's easy for the most important information to get lost. The result is confusion on the part of your prospect as they are trying to make sense of all the information you've communicated.

Now that you know this, you can be more aware of how much you're speaking. Keep in mind that the person you're meeting with is also most comfortable when they get the opportunity to speak about what they are passionate about. So resist the temptation to talk too much about your product or service early in the relationship, and focus on the prospect in front of you.

Number 2: You sound just like your competition.

You show up for a meeting with a prospect and communicate in a way that sounds and looks just like your competition. As human beings, we're constantly looking for outliers: Things that are different or unique in our environment. It's a survival mechanism so that we can quickly identify things that don't belong and then rightly categorize them as a danger or not. In a selling conversation when you sound just like the last salesperson who walked through your prospect's door, it makes it very difficult for your prospect to remember what is said, what's unique, or what's important about your product or service.

The other place this shows up is on your website. With a never-ending number of different companies within industries, it's interesting that you could look at two competing websites and swap the names of the companies on the website and not be able to tell the difference. You'll learn later in the book how to identify your unique value and highlight it in your conversations and your website so that you don't sound and look like your competition.

Number 3: The conversation is all about you.

The third behavior is the most damaging: Making the conversation all about you. Again, there is some simple psychology behind this. As human beings, we look at and view the world from our own perspective. This can lead you to communicating about your product or service from your point of view, rather than the prospect's. That's why the focus is on information about the company, product, or service. The prospect doesn't really care about this information early in the relationship. They care about the problems they face and the positive outcomes that you potentially can create for them.

Here's a more subtle aspect of the conversation being about the salesperson: Commissions. Have you ever met with a prospect and started to calculate what the commission would be for the sale? Or even worse, start to imagine what you'd spend the commission on?

You've been on the receiving end of this behavior. A salesperson is speaking with you, and you start to get the impression that they see dollar signs dancing over your head. It appears the sole focus of the conversation is to figure out how they can get those dollars into their back pocket. It's obvious that they only care about executing a sale.

Here's an extreme example of this behavior. A prospect receives a flier or email outlining the sales award trip to Hawaii that the salesperson would qualify for if they just got one more sale from the prospect. Yes, this really happens.

These types of behaviors can create a conversation that comes across as self-serving. Again, we've all experienced an interaction with a salesperson where, at the end of the conversation, they share with us the deal is only good until the end of the day. Or we may be faced with some other artificial inducement to try to get us to make a decision sooner than we're ready. This type of behavior is what has led to the used car salesman tag that can frequently get associated with any salesperson.

Here's an interesting tidbit about commissions. Daniel Pink in his book *Drive* (2011) shares insights on what motivates people. He cited research that proved a straight salary salesperson will out-perform a salesperson whose compensation has any commission associated with it. Sounds counterintuitive, doesn't it?

Here's why the salaried salesperson outperforms the commissioned salesperson: They are free to focus on the prospect without any thought of what it means to them. These three behaviors of a salesperson behaving badly are highlighted in a funny *Saturday Night Live* skit about a gentleman walking into a Verizon Cellular store (*Saturday Night Live* 2012). As soon as he walks into the store, he is greeted by a salesperson who immediately starts sharing with him exciting information about the devices in the store. He gives the customer all the speeds and feeds and techno jargon that you would expect if you were speaking to somebody in the cellular industry.

Early in the conversation, the customer asks a question, and the salesperson blows right through it and doesn't even acknowledge the question. He then goes on to paint a couple scenarios where the customer could be using a smartphone for his business and his personal life, all to which the customer's response is "no, thank you." After about two minutes of listening to everything that they wouldn't want to know about cellular technology, the customer walks out in frustration.

The important question that gets asked very early in this exchange is, "What does that mean?" When the customer asks this question, "What does this mean?" he literally is just trying to understand what it is that the salesperson was saying. But this question can live on two different levels.

One level is simply to understand what is being said.

The more important level is when a prospect or customer is trying to understand what your product or service means to them. Any time you're talking about your product or service, you can imagine a cartoon bubble over the head of your prospect that asks, "What does this mean to me?" That's what they are always thinking regardless of whether they ever ask that question out loud.

> *Any time you're talking about your product or service, you can imagine a cartoon bubble over the head of your prospect that asks, "What does this mean to me?" That's what they are always thinking regardless of whether they ever ask that question out loud.*

Let's look at an example of a business professional who behaves the right way.

There is a YouTube video that was released years ago that is about a blind man sitting in a park. As the video opens, you can see people walking past the blind man who's sitting on a mat. On his right is a tin can with a sign behind it that says, *"I'm blind, please help."*

You'll notice as people walk by every now and then, they'll stop and throw some coins on the mat or in the tin cup. After a few seconds of this, a woman walks by, looks at the blind man, and then turns back and picks up the sign. After a few minutes of writing on the back of the sign, she places it back and walks away. In the very next scene, you can see almost everyone who walks by is now dropping coins or bills onto the mat and into the tin cup. A little more time passes, and the woman comes back, and the blind man reaches out and touches her shoes, rightly identifying her as the individual who changed the sign. He looks up at her and asks, "What did you do to my sign?" She looks at him and says, "I wrote the same words but better."

> *Human beings make decisions based on meaning and emotion and justify our decisions with logic and reason.*

As she walks away, the camera pans out so that you can see that the sign now says, *"It's a beautiful day and I can't see it"* (Power of Words 2010).

Feel the difference?

The first sign is simply a statement of fact. The second sign is more about meaning and emotion. She changed the words so that as people walk by and read, "It's a beautiful day and I can't see it," they experience the meaning and associated emotion of what it *means* to be blind. As a result, the people who passed by dropped more money onto the mat (Power of Words 2010).

Antonio Damasio, a noted neuroscientist, proved what we've long suspected about human behavior.

Human beings make decisions based on meaning and emotion and justify our decisions with logic and reason.

Some of you who are reading this are going to want to challenge the previous statement. You're probably similar to the Oracle consultant I ran across in a workshop with about twenty of his peers.

During the workshop I made the same statement that

> **Human beings make decisions based on meaning and emotion and justify our decisions with logic and reason.**

you just read a few sentences ago: people make decisions based on meaning and emotion and justify the decision with logic and reason.

When I made that statement, he raised his hand. I asked him if he had a question. He said he didn't have a question, but that he disagreed with what I had just said. He went on to explain that he was one of the most logical people you'd ever meet. As a matter of fact, he believed he was so logical that he would make Mr. Spock look like an emotional mess. In the moment, I made a split-second decision.

I asked him, "When was the last important buying decision that you made for you or your family?" He thought about it for a minute and answered that he had purchased a new car about six months ago. At this point, I asked him to give me an opportunity to run a quick experiment with him and the rest of the team.

I turned to his peers, and I asked them to put on their logic-and-reason hat. While applying just logic and reason, I asked them to give me the makes and models of cars that they would buy if it were purely a logical exercise. They started sharing cars like Honda Accord, Toyota Prius, Volvo, Camry, and cars that would be low cost to run and maintain and would last a long time. While they were sharing these different makes and models, I noticed that the body language of the consultant who had raised his hand had changed dramatically. It looked like he was trying to disappear out of his seat.

I then turned back to him and asked if he would be willing to share with his peers the car he had purchased. He shared that he had bought a BMW.

He then threw up his hands and said, "All right, all right! You're right, it was an emotional decision, but I got a great deal!" A great deal: There is the logical justification for his emotional purchase. BMW commercials are all about immersing the viewer in this experience that they can have when driving a BMW, obviously playing on the viewer's emotions. They know this will lead to more consumers purchasing their cars.

This gentleman made the same mistake that a lot of us do when it comes to decision-making. In Daniel Kahneman's book, *Thinking, Fast and Slow* (2015), he discusses the two different levels of consciousness and decision-making. What many of us don't realize is that we make decisions subconsciously that we're not even aware of. This can lead us to believe that the decisions are only being made from our conscious mind and are mostly logical.

Let's look at an example. I'm sure there's times where you've been driving and realize that you've mentally checked out and have been daydreaming about some other topic. This may go on for several miles while you are driving your car, not realizing that you're not actively paying attention to the driving. The reason for this is that driving has become so second-nature that you're doing it subconsciously. There are a lot of split-second, individual decisions that it takes to navigate a car on the road.

This also happens in a buying decision. We can make a snap judgment or decision subconsciously and not even realize that we bypassed the logical part of our decision-making.

Going back to the YouTube video about the blind man, it's obvious to see that the individuals walking by were responding to the second sign because of the emotion and meaning evoked by those words (Power of Words 2010).

You have the same opportunity to communicate with your prospects and customers in a way that they under-stand the meaning for them and experience the corresponding emotion.

How does all this play into developing a winning mindset?

There's a simple question that you can ask yourself before you ever engage in a conversation with a prospect or customer to ensure that you have the right mindset—a winning mindset. This question showed up in a workshop I did for a software company in Atlanta.

The COO of this company was heading up a two-day sales kickoff and had asked me to facilitate a half-day workshop on the second day. She spoke during the lunch session of the second day and was covering revenue goals for the upcoming year. At the end of her session, she put a slide up that said $88.8 million. She then looked at the room and said the most important thing for everyone in the room was how they were going to contribute the $88.8 million revenue goal. She then concluded the talk and introduced me.

As I stood in front of the room, I said, "I have good news and bad news. The bad news is that the $88.8 million is not the most important thing for everyone. The most important thing is how they answer this question: *How is your prospect going to be better off as a result of doing business with you?*"

I assured them that if they could answer that question with honesty and integrity, the good news was that they would blow past the $88.8 million revenue goal.

Making the answer to the question or the outcome they'll create for the prospect the primary focus creates a North Star effect on the relationship. Now the focus is squarely on helping the prospect realize this outcome, which aligns the seller's intentions with the buyer's.

By having the answer to that question as your focal point, there's another benefit for you as a salesperson. In conversations with sales professionals and listening to some of the answers that they come up with, it's not uncommon to hear things like: "My prospect will have peace of mind;" "My prospect will be able to spend more time on things that they enjoy;" or "They'll be able to focus their time and energy on things that will have a bigger impact on their business."

When I asked the salesperson how creating those outcomes for their prospects makes them feel, the obvious answer is it feels good. Part of developing a winning mindset is being clear about *why* you're selling a product or service.

If the answer is only to make money, that will only take you so far. If your "why" is to have a positive impact on another human being, it can have a ripple effect on your behavior. All of a sudden, cold calling isn't as much of a challenge because you're focused on how you can impact someone else's life. Every activity necessary to create a customer now has new meaning.

Take a minute to review the following example to see how it feels to approach sales with this winning mindset.

Example

In this example, we'll reflect how it may sound to craft the benefits you offer to a company through selling your product. ERP Software Company will be our example company and discussed throughout the book.

ERP Software Company will benefit because:

- Their prospects will have more time to spend on activities that will advance their business.

- Their prospects will have the insights they need to increase profits.

- Their prospects will provide better service to their clients.

CHAPTER 2

MASTER THE SCIENCE OF DECISION

Now that you've learned about developing a winning mindset and how humans make decisions, you will next learn more about the science of decision and other principles and techniques you can utilize in your conversations to ensure that you're communicating high value in a way that's clear and easy to understand. To accomplish this, we'll cover:

1. The three major parts of the brain and the role they play in decisions.
2. The importance of meaning, emotion, logic, and reason.
3. SUCCESS: a checklist to ensure you're speaking the language of decision.
4. The role of hormones in a selling conversation.

Decisions and the Brain

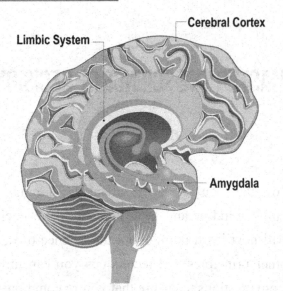

It's important to have a basic understanding of decision-making as it relates to the human brain. There are three major parts of the brain: the cerebral cortex, the limbic system, and the amygdala. We'll look closely at the role that each of these parts of the brain play when a human being is trying to make a decision.

Cerebral Cortex

The cerebral cortex is the largest part of the human brain. It's the wrinkled outermost portion of the brain. Its function and role are focused primarily on logic and reason. Think of it as the onboard computer for the human brain. The cerebral cortex is responsible for executive function, language, memory, and a whole host of high-level processing and thinking.

Limbic System

The limbic system is a smaller part of the brain underneath the cerebral cortex. The limbic system is where all our emotions reside. Love, hate, fear, passion—just about any human emotion that you can imagine comes from and is experienced through the limbic system.

What the limbic system does not possess is the ability for speech. That's a function of the cerebral cortex. It's why when you've made a decision and you get asked to explain that decision, often times you're left with a loss of words.

A great example of this would be when I proposed to my wife over thirty years ago. At the time, the friends that I was hanging out with wanted to understand how I had come to this most important decision. My answer wasn't, "I developed a spreadsheet with thirty of the most important criteria for the perfect spouse, and my wife had the highest score of any woman that I had dated." The actual response was I just knew in my heart of hearts that this was the right decision. Other phrases that you might hear would be, "I know in my gut," "I just have a feeling," "I have a knowing," or any number of similar explanations. Again, this is a demonstration of the decisions that are being made emotionally in the limbic system that we have no language to explain.

An interesting fact about the limbic system is that it's more active in teenagers and people over seventy. The reason it's more active in teenagers, which explains why teenagers say stupid things and often make questionable decisions, is because the cerebral cortex is not completely formed in a human being until they're around 25 years old. This means for teenagers the limbic system is more dominant, which can explain why parents of teenagers will often comment that they believe that their teenager is brain damaged. It's not actually brain damage; it's the fact that the cerebral cortex part of the brain is not completely formed.

The limbic system also starts to take dominance as people get older. I experienced this with my father as he hit his seventies. I'd notice the way that he would interact with our children, and it was nothing like the way that he interacted with me as a child. He was much stricter and a disciplinarian with me; but when watching him interact with my kids, I've noticed that he's very quick to emotion and tears. As a matter of fact, I caught him watching a Dove commercial and no more than five or ten seconds into the commercial, it was obvious that it was impacting him emotionally because of the tears coming down his face.

Amygdala

The amygdala sits at the base of the brain and is connected to the spinal cord. The amygdala is responsible for our survival on planet Earth. It is the flight-or-fight mechanism that we experience when we're confronted with something that the amygdala believes to be dangerous.

It's constantly surveying the environment that we are in to determine if we're safe or not. Think of it this way: It's a binary switch. The first decision it must make is if you are safe or not. When it believes it is in danger, then the next binary decision is if you fight or if you run.

When you look at how these three parts of the brain work together, it's easy to see why the amygdala is connected to the spinal column. The spinal column is responsible for providing input to the brain specifically around your five senses. The brain is constantly receiving information from the spinal cord involving sight, touch, smell, taste, and sound.

The first part of the brain to receive this information is the amygdala. This makes perfect sense. The amygdala has priority over all the other parts of the brain because it needs to make an instantaneous decision as to your safety. That's why it gets first access to this information from the spinal cord.

The second part of the brain that gets this information is the limbic system. At this point, the limbic brain is trying to determine how it feels about the information that it's receiving.

The last part of the brain that gets information from the spinal cord is the cerebral cortex. At this point, the cerebral cortex is trying to figure out what it thinks about the information that it has received.

Looking at this, it's easy to see how the brain processes information. Based on the information provided by the five senses, you make decisions first around your safety, then how you feel about the information, and lastly, how you think about the information. You literally make decisions from the inside-out. Yet when you look at the majority of selling conversations, the focus is on making a logical argument for why an individual should purchase a product or service. Typically, there's very little focus around emotion or safety that would speak to both the amygdala and the limbic system.

Focusing more on the function of the limbic system, Antonio Damasio, an Italian behavioral psychologist, discovered the importance of emotion in decision-making. In working with a patient who had damage to the limbic part of the brain, he observed how difficult it was for this individual to make a decision. In this initial study, Damasio realized that his patient could explain the pros and cons of a specific decision, but when it came time to choosing, he was unable to do so. Damasio expanded his research to other individuals who also had experienced damage to the limbic part of the brain. In these studies, he would give them a simple choice for lunch, whether they would have peanut butter and jelly or a bologna sandwich. Again, the subjects he was studying could explain their preference or a logical reason for choosing one or the other, but when it came time to make a decision, they were unable to (Purves *et al.* 2001).

The scientific proof behind the fact that we make decisions based on meaning and emotion leads to this question:

How do you address this in the conversations you're having with your prospects and customers?

Speaking the Language of Decision

Speaking the language of decision in the conversations you have with your prospects and customers is essential to successful selling. The next seven concepts can be used as a checklist to ensure that you're speaking in a way that makes it easy for your prospects and customers to understand what your product means to them, so they can more easily make a decision. Keep in mind that using these principles does not mean if you construct your conversations according to them you'll see below that you'll always get a "yes." Instead, they allow you to communicate with your prospects and customers in a way that makes it easy for them to say yes or no.

Simple

Keep the words and concepts that you use in a conversation simple. The ability to take complicated concepts and ideas and communicate them in a way that is simple is an important element of being successful. It is a sign of higher emotional intelligence. It's the ability to take complex concepts and make them simple. This is especially true in communicating with prospects and customers. Stay away from words and concepts that would lead your prospect to ask the question, "What does this mean?"

If you do get that question in a conversation, pay attention to what you just said that caused your prospect to ask what you mean. What you'll typically find yourself doing is answering them with an analogy or metaphor that they're familiar with to create understanding. In the future, use that same analogy or metaphor with other prospects to explain the concept you're trying to communicate instead of what you previously used that caused confusion.

Unexpected

John Medina (2009) identified ten basic principles as to how the human brain works. One of the things that he discovered is that the human attention span (when somebody is presenting or communicating to them) is roughly around seven to ten minutes. What this means is in a presentation when you're communicating information around your product or service, after about seven minutes, you're at risk of losing the attention of your audience. The explanation behind this is that the amygdala has determined that it is safe in this type of meeting. When the amygdala determines that it's safe, it causes the person's brain to check out. They may start to think about emails that need to be returned, dinner that needs to be cooked, or children who need to be picked up at school. This is not the kind of behavior that you're looking for in a sales presentation.

What Medina discovered is that there are ways to hook your prospect or customer's attention by doing something unexpected. There are a number of techniques that you can use in a conversation that would fall into the unexpected category.

Here's a quick example. If you were to start a meeting with a high-level, quick overview of your company, one way of doing that would be to write three numbers on a whiteboard. You can introduce the three numbers by saying, "There's an interesting story around these three numbers 25, 80, 99." You could then go on to share that the twenty-five represents the number of years that you've been in business, eighty represents 80% of the fortune 250 are your customers, and ninety-nine means that 99% of your customers gave you a high customer satisfaction score.

When you use a "number-play" and write three numbers up on a board and say that there's an interesting story behind those three numbers, it immediately creates intrigue in the amygdala. The amygdala immediately recognizes that it doesn't understand or know the riddle behind the three numbers. It may be thinking the numbers could mean twenty-five fire trucks outside, eighty police cars, and a 99% chance it survives the burning building it's in. The amygdala will pay attention up to the point that it can determine that it's safe. This type of technique not only engages your audience but also ensures that they'll remember the most important things that you have to share. We'll dive into other techniques you can use that would fall under the category of unexpected.

Concrete

With concrete versus abstract, you want to stay away from abstract concepts and ideas. Again, you'll know that you're being abstract if a prospect or customer asks you what you mean. Let's look at an example of abstract where someone uses the word justice in a presentation. Some people in the room would be thinking justice of the peace, the person sitting in black robes in a courtroom. Other people will think of "justice" scale. More people may be thinking of justice versus mercy. Then the justice that they were actually referring to could have been David Justice who hit a home run to win the World Series for the Atlanta Braves in 1995.

In contrast, if you were to say the word "elephant," everybody in the room would have the same mental image of a big gray pachyderm. There would be no guessing, and everybody would be on the same page. That's an example of a word or concept that is concrete. To the best of your ability, use words or concepts that are concrete—or words and ideas that can't be quickly interpreted in many different ways—for the audience that you're speaking to.

Contrast

Think about this question: How does a human being perceive value?

Typical answers would be: It's different for each person; it's about the benefit to an individual; or it revolves around the relationship of price to benefit. These and any other number of explanations would be what you would expect to hear.

There's a behavioral psychologist who won a Nobel Prize in 2002 in economics. Think about that fact. A behavioral psychologist wins the most prestigious award in economics. The reason for this recognition is that he cracked the code on how human beings perceive value.

His name is Daniel Kahneman. He's best known for the book mentioned earlier named *Thinking, Fast and Slow*. In his book, he dives into great detail about the science of decision.

Value is perceived in a contrasting worldview. Literally, it's the contrast between, "this is what your world looks like without a product or service" versus "this is what your world could look like with a product or service." It's in the side-by-side comparison that human beings perceive value. Here's an example:

Think about the world that you live in without air conditioning: Driving to work in sweltering heat and humidity; walking into an office only supplied with fans; and spending the day in a suit and tie in unbearable heat. This was the reality before the 1950s.

Now contrast that with the world that we live in today. In the middle of summer when it's hot and humid and you find yourself walking inside to an air-conditioned room, you experience instant value in the contrast between hot, humid air and dry, cool air. Keep in mind the contrast must be immediate. If you walked inside the building and had to wait a couple of hours for the air to be cooled, the value would not be the same.

There's a formula you can use to determine the perceived value for your product and service as it relates to your prospect. It shows up in the diagram below.

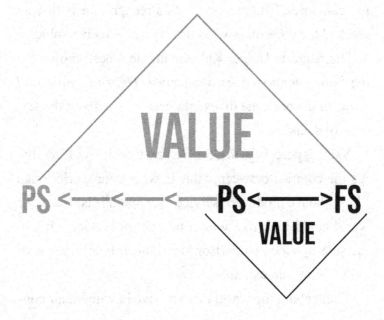

Formula that determines Perceived Value (gray) is
Future State (FS) - Present State (PS) = Value (black).

Any time you start a conversation with a prospect, they have an understanding of their present state. The present state would be what their world looks like today, the challenges they face, and the impact or consequences of those challenges. You show up and you start talking about your products and services, and they start to imagine what their future state would look like. It's the gap between these two worldviews where they experience value.

However, most prospects don't really understand the impact of their present state. This gives you an opportunity to ask questions that cause them to understand that the challenges they face today are actually worse than what they had imagined. By asking these questions, their understanding of their present state starts to move to the left, and now when you flip the conversation to describe the future state, the perceived value is much higher.

So the formula that determines the perceived value is Future State (FS) - Present State (PS) = Value.

As a salesperson, it's on you to communicate in a way that creates this contrasting worldview. This creates the highest perceived value of your product or service with your prospects. The opportunity to do this shows up in every conversation that you would have with your prospects. You can also use this technique in different mediums that you would use to communicate. This includes your website, emails, cold calls, first conversation, demonstrations, and proposals.

Emotion

You've already read where emotion plays a role in decision-making, but there's another dynamic important to emotion.

As you're reading this book, I'd like you to think about what happened years ago on 9/11. For those who are old enough to remember where they were and what they were doing, those details are forever seared into their memory.

However, if you asked the same person what they had for lunch two weeks ago, they probably can't remember.

The reason that they can remember in detail what happened around 9/11 is because of the emotions associated with the memory. That's also the reason why they couldn't remember what they had for lunch two weeks ago. There was no strong emotion associated with their lunch.

Emotion leads to detailed memory.

The stronger the emotion, the more detailed the memory. It's a survival mechanism in your brain. Any time you experience a strong, painful emotion, your brain releases hormones to create detailed memory around what happened right before, during, and after the event. It's the brain's way of creating a memory so that if you ever see those details again, you know to move away from that scenario or situation.

Memory is also created around positive emotions. Think back to some of the more positive memories you've experienced. It could be the birth of a child, your wedding, or some other positive significant event that has happened in your life. Again, it's your brain's way of creating detailed memory around what happened before, during, and after the event. This way if you ever see that scenario or those details again, you know that it's safe to move toward that thing or event.

If you want your prospects and customers to remember the conversations that you're having with them, there needs to be some element of emotion. One of the strongest human emotions is pain. This is why it's important to ask questions that cause your prospect to experience the reality and pain of their current situation. The more pain (or mental suffering) they experience in the conversation, the more likely they are to remember the conversation. And don't worry; this isn't to torture the prospect. Since you are providing a possible solution to that suffering through your product or service, now they see the true value of what you have to offer.

Sight

Out of your five senses, sight is the most important for survival. If you were to go on an expedition to India and explore some of their jungles where Bengal tigers live, and you can only keep one of your five senses, which one would you keep? The right answer or most common answer is sight. John Medina found that vision engages over 70% of your brain. The reason for this is obvious: You depend on your sight more than any of the other four senses (2009).

Medina also found something significant about sight as it relates to selling conversations. If you have a verbal conversation with a prospector or customer, the best-case scenario is that two days later they'll remember about 20% of what was said. However, if you associate a picture or an image with the conversation, two days later they will remember over 70% of what is said (2009).

Think about the way that you recall memories. When somebody asks you to remember something, you don't pull up a tickertape of words that were said in a conversation. You start to envision the memory, a picture or image associated with the memory, and then also remember how you felt about that memory. As human beings, we recall memories through images, not words.

This is why it's important to associate images or pictures with the conversations you're having with your prospects and customers. It gives them the best opportunity to remember the conversation and the most important points made during the conversation. Later in the book, you'll discover several techniques that you can use to associate images with your conversations.

Story

Story is an important element of selling, and you'll read later in the book how to incorporate specific stories in your selling conversations. Stories will help you connect more emotionally with your prospects.

Hormones

There are three major hormones that come into play in any relationship, especially a sales relationship. These hormones affect the way that people feel in a relationship and during a conversation.

Cortisol

Cortisol is commonly referred to as the stress hormone. It shows up in a flight-or-fight situation, readying our bodies to either run or fight. In this scenario, it's perfectly normal for cortisol to exist, but outside of this scenario, cortisol can have a negative impact on human beings.

The most common challenge that cortisol is associated with is weight gain. If we experience a high level of stress day in and day out, cortisol can start to impact not only our weight, but our health overall. Stress has been linked to conditions like high blood pressure, high cholesterol, and other medical conditions that could be quite dangerous for a human being.

Where cortisol can show up in a sales conversation is when a salesperson tries to take control of the conversation. This can show up in a number of ways. It could be the hard close at the end of a conversation or a subtle form of manipulation that a salesperson might use in holding out a deal that is only good for a 24-hour period.

The common thread of behaviors exhibited by a salesperson that can produce cortisol in your prospect or customer is when the prospect feels like they are not the primary focus of the salesperson. When this happens, the prospect experiences cortisol and will try to find a way out of the conversation as quickly as possible. Additionally, they are completely closed off to new ways of thinking or new ways of solving some of their challenges. This is the exact opposite of the type of behavior you would want of a prospect in a selling conversation. Ideally, you'd like them to be open to suggestions and new ideas so that they will consider changing the way that they do things today and adopt a new approach associated with your product or service.

There is an exception where cortisol is a good thing in a selling conversation. It's when you're speaking to the challenges or problems the prospect is trying to solve. In this case, you want them to experience a elevated level of stress associated with the challenge. You want them to feel the impact of the challenge so that they are open to ideas that will move them away from the pain.

Dopamine

Dopamine is a feel-good hormone. Unfortunately, the effect or impact of dopamine is short-lived. Some common scenarios when you experience dopamine would be checking off an item of your to-do list; completing a project or task around the house; or, in the sales world, when you get a prospect to agree to move forward as a client and close a deal. All those scenarios cause dopamine to drip on your brain and make you feel good momentarily.

The more common experience with dopamine is associated with your smartphones. When you create a Facebook post and people start to comment on or like what you posted, your brain has learned to cause dopamine to drip, which makes you feel good. This is true when you receive an email or text. Anything that makes your smartphone buzz, vibrate, or ring will cause dopamine to be released in your brain. Unfortunately, this has led to a lot of the behavior that we see around smartphones. We've essentially become addicted to a dopamine drip as we carry around these devices that are constantly letting us know that we are important, loved, or appreciated.

This can show up even more dramatically when someone who carries their smartphone in their pocket one day finds themselves without it. A common phenomenon in this situation is that the person still experiences a vibration where the smartphone would normally be. It's the brain's way of tricking them so that it can release dopamine that would normally be associated with a real vibration from a smartphone in a pocket.

Dopamine is one of the underlying reasons why it's so difficult for people to disengage from these amazing devices. It causes a smartphone addiction.

Look again where dopamine shows up in a selling relationship. Imagine you just spent many days, weeks, or months working with a prospective client and finally the day is here when they're ready to sign on the dotted line. When that happens, dopamine floods your brain in a way that makes you feel a sense of satisfaction and well-being. The problem is that the customer sitting across from the table signing on the dotted line will be experiencing some level of cortisol (meaning stress). They realize that there are several excellent reasons why they should do business with you to solve some of the challenges and problems that they face; but in agreeing to do business with you, they're also agreeing to change the way that they do things today.

Contemplating change almost always introduces some amount of cortisol or stress. It's important to keep this in mind so that you can do everything in your power to assure your new client that the change will be as minimal and as painless as possible. Some of the common ways you can do this is to offer case studies, customer testimonials, and any information that would continue to reinforce the positive outcomes that they're going to be experiencing in doing business with you.

Oxytocin

Oxytocin is the trust hormone. When oxytocin is present in two human beings, it's causing both of those individuals to experience a sense of trust, connection, and belonging.

The most common occurrence of the highest concentration of oxytocin in a human being is when a mother gives birth to a child. At the moment that this happens, when the child is born, oxytocin floods both the mother and child. This is what creates this amazing bond between mother and baby.

As a matter of fact, in today's world, it's more and more common for when a baby is born to not only spend time bonding with the mother, but also creating ways for oxytocin to be present in the father and baby. The way that this happens is for the father to take off his shirt and to hold the baby skin-to-skin and in his arms. This has been shown to release not quite the same high levels of oxytocin as with the mother, but still a significant amount to create a bond between the father and newborn baby.

Obviously in a sales relationship, a salesperson would like to elicit trust and belonging with their prospects and customers. There are a number of ways to ensure that oxytocin is present in this type of relationship.

Eye Contact

Making eye contact with another human being is one way to elicit the release of oxytocin. However, there is a degree of eye contact that you want to maintain in a conversation. If you're meeting somebody for the first time and you're just starting to establish a relationship, eye contact should only be maintained about half of the time. Once the relationship has been established, then eye contact between the two of you most of the time is more natural. Nobody enjoys or appreciates constant eye contact for the whole conversation. That just comes across as creepy and, even worse, potentially intimidating.

Touch

As you've already read, a skin-to-skin connection between mother and baby and father and baby is one way that oxytocin is released in this new relationship. The same is true for human beings in general. Anytime you have skin-to-skin contact with another human being, oxytocin will be released. The reason for this is that the brain recognizes if you are in close proximity with another human being, they must be safe. With close proximity for a handshake, the brain registers this closeness as safety and as a trigger to recognize that this person can be trusted. Otherwise, you would never get that close to another human if it wasn't obvious that you would be safe with that person.

Touch in a professional relationship can show up in a handshake, or in some cases a hug. Recognizing that not everybody is comfortable with hugs, you need to be certain that the person that you would hug in a professional setting would be okay with it. That said, handshakes are always acceptable and should be utilized in any relationship. Every time you join hands with another human being, oxytocin is released.

Mirroring

Mirroring is the unconscious mimicking or copying of another human's behavior. As you spend time together with people that you trust, you'll observe mirroring. When you're out to dinner with friends or family, watch what happens when one individual in the group picks up their glass of water to take a sip. Very quickly, you'll see a number of people at the table also pick up a water glass and take a sip. This type of mimicking can show up in speech patterns, body movement, and several other physical behaviors. In most cases, people are completely unconscious to the fact that they are mirroring another individual. It's a way to signal between two human beings that they belong together or that they're like each other.

Mirroring can also be done intentionally. Specifically, to elicit the release of oxytocin and create a bond of trust with another human being. An example of this could show up the next time you get together with a friend or co-worker for a cup of coffee. Try this quick experiment: Wait until the person that you're having coffee with has an empty coffee cup. Pick up your coffee cup and take a sip. Watch to see how long it takes the person with the empty coffee cup to pick the cup up and put it to their lips. In some cases, even after they've recognized that the cup is empty, they will mirror you again the next time you pick up your cup.

Now that you understand this behavior, pay close attention to the ways that your friends and family mirror each other when they are together.

There has been a lot written over the years on how to adapt your conversation and behavior depending on the personality type of your prospect. Take DISC personality testing for example: If you pick up on the fact that your prospect is a Driver, you know to behave a certain way.

The challenge with this approach is that you can be more focused on trying to determine their personality style and miss what's really important: Paying attention to your prospect. Mirroring is an easier way to adapt to the personality type or style of the person that you're trying to build a relationship with.

If the person that you're meeting with is a fast talker, pick up your pace of speech. If they are a slow talker, then slow the pace of your speech. If they behave in a way where they come across as a bottom-line individual, then your conversation and conduct should mirror that. Make sure that you provide short and succinct answers to questions. If they come across as a detail-oriented person, then provide more detail than you might normally provide in your conversation.

Body language is another easy way to mirror the individuals you're meeting with. If you're sitting across the desk from a prospect and they lean back, you lean back. If they lean forward and cross their hands, you can lean forward and cross your hands. One of the side benefits of this type of technique is that you're becoming more focused and in-tune with the prospect.

You may be wondering if this type of behavior will be picked up by your prospect or customer. It's very rare that this would ever happen unless you're overexaggerating your behavior. Again, mirroring is a subconscious behavior that most of us do normally, so when it's done intentionally, it doesn't stand out as abnormal.

Eye contact, touch, and mirroring can happen naturally in a face-to-face meeting. This is why it's important to meet your prospects in person, if at all possible, especially in a world that is relying on web meetings more and more to facilitate sales. Obviously, there are some sales that make more sense for the phone or web. Typically, it's a product or service that doesn't cost a lot. As the price tag goes up, so does the need to establish trust with your prospect. You'll have to decide where the tipping point is for your product or service. At a minimum, take advantage of the camera on your laptop or phone when meeting with a prospect virtually. At least you'll be able to establish eye contact and some mirroring.

The number one way to elicit oxytocin in a relationship with your prospect or customer showed up in a question you read in chapter 1. The question was, "How is your prospect going to be better off as a result of doing business with you?"

When your focus is completely on your prospect and your ability to help them in their role or career, this elicits oxytocin because the person that you're interacting with feels like you're in it for them. Oxytocin is released any time you help another person, and they sense that there's no ulterior motive.

> *When your focus is completely on your prospect and your ability to help them in their role or career, this elicits oxytocin because the person that you're interacting with feels like you're in it for them.*

Think back to the blind man in the park. Did the woman who changed the sign have an ulterior motive? Did she whisper to the blind man, "Hey when I come back, I want 25 percent of the increased giving as a result of me changing the sign"? Probably not. Since the blind man knew there was nothing he could do for the woman, he had an implicit sense of trust. On the other side of the equation, the woman had a sense of fulfillment and connectedness to the man she just helped. Both were experiencing oxytocin.

You and your prospects can experience the same dynamic.

This type of giving is discussed at length in Adam Grant's book, *Give and Take* (2014). He studies the different types of reciprocity styles that individuals operate in the business world. The three styles that he discusses are a taker, matcher, or giver. In starting the research associated with this book, he assumed that the takers would always have more success than the other two reciprocity styles. It seemed fairly logical that individuals who are completely focused on themselves would always do things that are in their best interest. This would then cause them to have more success in their career than the other two reciprocity styles.

What he found in his research surprised him. He found that givers, in the short-term, would lag behind in their respective careers. Typically, this is because they are looking for ways to help their peers, even to the detriment of their own initial success. But over time, the givers would outperform the takers and the matchers. The only exception to this is when givers are not self-aware enough to recognize when they're being taken advantage of (Grant 2014).

The moral of the story is that when we put others' interests ahead of our own, like in a selling relationship, it causes the release of oxytocin and a high degree of trust. That is why the answer to the question, "How is your prospect going to be better off as a result of doing business with you?" is so important. When you focus on that outcome as the reason why you want to do business with a prospect, they get a sense that you have their best interest at heart. This creates a strong bond of trust.

CHAPTER 3

CREATE VALUE POSITIONS, NOT VALUE PROPOSITIONS

Value positions are the building blocks for any customer-facing communication, so you will next learn how to identify your value positions in the marketplace.

To accomplish this, we'll cover:

1. Why versus meaning.
2. The role of value positions in B2C and B2B.
3. How to identify your ideal customer persona (ICP).
4. The challenges you must understand.
5. Where you are unique or strong.
6. You-phrasing and Value Position Statements (VPS).

Why Versus Meaning

In his book, *Start with Why* (2011), Simon Sinek unpacks why some companies have wild success in the face of stiff competition. As a noted marketer, years ago he decided to decode why some companies have more success in a commoditized market. His goal was to do this in a way that would be very simple and easy to understand. This is the genesis of the Golden Circle that appears in *Start with Why*. See the diagram below.

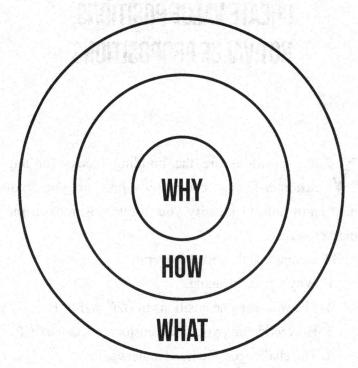

What Simon found is that most companies are clear on *what* they deliver in the way of a product or service and *how* they go about doing that. But what he discovered is that it's the most successful companies that are clear about *why* they are in business.

In the book, he focused on three examples: Starbucks, Southwest Airlines, and Apple. He found that all three companies in a very commoditized market are able to achieve extraordinary success because they're very clear about their *why*.

The story behind Starbucks is that Howard Schultz, the CEO and founder of Starbucks, took a trip to Italy back in the 70s. During that trip, he experienced the amazing culture of the Italians, especially the prevalence of cafes wherever he traveled. What he learned is that the Italians have three places where they hang out: home, work, and the cafes. The cafes are a place where the community gathers throughout the course of the day to hang out with friends and family over coffee, snacks, or, later in the day, wine. The cafes are the third place where Italians spend time.

During his travels in Italy, Howard decided to create a third place to spend time in the United States: A place for people to hang out and socialize in much the same way that they do in the cafes in Italy. If you were to ask a Starbucks barista the *why* behind Starbucks, the majority of them would answer, "To be third place." It sounds funny for somebody to say that they want to be third place, but this means they literally want to create a third place where people can go and socialize to hang out over coffee.

It's interesting in Starbucks establishing their *why*, the focus was not on selling more coffee than any other coffee shop in the U.S. Everybody within Starbucks from the CEO on down is very clear about their *why*. It is to create an environment for people in the U.S. to experience community in the form of a coffee shop. The coffee and other things that are sold are merely there to help create this environment.

Southwest Airlines was created back in the seventies when 80% of all air travel was experienced by business professionals. Herb Keller, the CEO and founder of Southwest Airlines, recognized this fact and established the *why* of Southwest Airlines. It is to make air travel affordable for everybody within the United States. The employees of Southwest Airlines are so clear about the *why* that when customers suggest to the flight attendants that they would like more meal choices, the flight attendants know how to deal with this request. It is to ask themselves, "Is this going to help us make air travel more affordable?" If the answer is no, then they know not to run this type of idea up the chain of command. Again, the sole focus of Southwest Airlines is to make air travel affordable for everybody.

The culture that they created and the success that they've had resulted in an amazing phenomena around 9/11. During the emotional crisis of 9/11, Southwest Airlines made the decision to communicate to their customers who had tickets that they could apply for a full refund. This put Southwest Airlines in a precarious position because if the majority of the customers asked for a refund, it could have financially crippled the company. Because of the reputation, experience, and culture that Southwest had established, their customers were so loyal that not only did they not request refunds, but some customers even sent money to Southwest Airlines so that they could stay afloat.

Apple's *why* is to challenge the status quo. Steve Jobs instilled in the Apple employees a mantra and desire to always look at the world and find a better way to do things. It's this type of culture that has revolutionized the music industry that we enjoy today. It shouldn't come as a surprise that Steve would bring this type of focus to Apple. He grew up in the 60s and 70s, which were all about doing things differently than the way our parents did.

The common theme across all three companies is that they are very clear about *why* they are in business. The *why* becomes a filter for making decisions about the future development of products and services for each company. Once a company is clear on their *why*, then they can determine *how* they create an experience with their customers that aligns with the *why*, and then *what* the product or service would be to create that experience.

Compare that to how other companies in those industries operate. For example, Delta created an airline called Song. The whole focus of creating Song was to replicate everything that they understood about Southwest Airlines. This includes a fun and light atmosphere created by the flight attendants, cheaper air fares, limited meals, and everything else that Southwest Airlines had put in place. However, there was one key element missing when Delta created Song. They didn't do it from the same *why* as Southwest Airlines. As a result, customers of

Song never really felt the reason that Delta created Song was to make air travel more affordable for customers in the United States. In essence, Delta's behavior with Song didn't align with their *why*, and customers were able to intuitively understand this. This resulted in Song going out of business within a couple of years of their launch (Sinek 2011).

Meaning is derived or experienced by your prospects and customers when you communicate outcomes that will make a difference in their work and lives.

So how does the *why* of a company impact the selling conversations that you have with your prospects and customers? Just like your *why* in your business is an indicator of success in the business world, there's a corresponding word that is an indicator of success in the selling conversations that you have with your prospects and customers.

You discovered this word earlier in the book but in different context. The word is *means* or *meaning*. There's a similar diagram you can use to ensure that you're clear on what your product means for your prospect or customer. See the diagram on the next page.

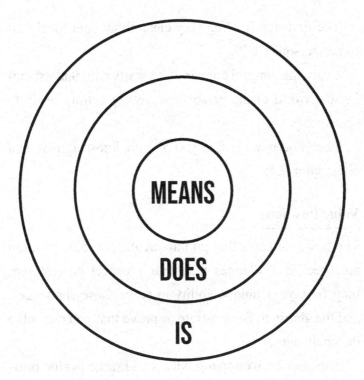

Instead of *why, how,* and *what,* the conversation in the Golden Circle is *means, does,* and *is.* Just like being clear about your *why* is an indicator of success for your company's product or service, being clear on what your product *means* to the prospect or customer will create success in the conversations that you're having with your prospects and customers.

Meaning is derived or experienced by your prospects and customers when you communicate outcomes that will make a difference in their work and lives. Outcomes have meaning, and meaning has corresponding emotions associated with them.

The first step is being very clear about your ideal customer persona (ICP).

Every meaningful conversation starts with understanding the world of the person that you're getting ready to speak to.

The good news is that you already know a great deal about your ICP.

Value Positions

The basic elements that go into creating a value position are specific challenges that your prospect or customer may face, your unique ability to solve those challenges, and the ability to demonstrate or prove that you can solve the challenges.

You may be wondering why it's phrased "value position" instead of "value proposition." When you look at the phrase "value proposition," *proposition* is a suggestion. If you look at the exact meaning of value proposition, you're suggesting to a prospect or customer that your product or service may have value. This begs the question, "Why don't you know if your product or service represents value to your prospect?" If you know, take a position around that value. That's a lot different than a proposition. By identifying a value *position*, you can stake out a position in the marketplace that represents real and unique value for your prospect.

Below you'll find the steps necessary to identify the elements that go into a value position. Then you'll see how you take those elements and create a value position statement that will be used in any customer or prospect-facing communication.

Goals

In thinking about your ICP, consider the goals and objectives that they're trying to accomplish in their respective roles. Over the next few paragraphs, you're going to see examples specific to a sales leader. As a sales professional, see how close the examples are to your world.

Sales leaders are responsible for generating revenue. But when you look at that, it's not just generating revenue, it's *how* they generate revenue.

Some corresponding goals associated with generating revenue could be how they onboard and hire team members, making sure that the team sells a healthy mix of products or services, or finding ways that their team can achieve success from top to bottom so that everybody is contributing. The bottom line is that it all comes back to hitting a revenue goal.

Challenges

Some of the common challenges that sales leaders face would include the 80/20 split in performance. It's when 80% of the revenue is generated by 20% of the sales team. This is a common phenomenon in a organization and represents a significant challenge for the sales leader in lifting the performance of the other 80%.

Another challenge would be the onboarding of a new salesperson. The sales leader and the corresponding number that they're chasing doesn't change based on the number of team members. So when they hire a new salesperson, it's critical that they are empowered to get up to speed and start generating revenue as quickly as possible.

Other challenges would be specific to the sales process itself, like having enough opportunities or new prospects for the team to engage. Or on the other side of the coin, converting those opportunities at a higher rate as they move through the sales process and sales funnel.

These and others represent significant challenges and obstacles for the sales leader.

Identifying Uniqueness and Your Strengths

Once you've identified common challenges that your ICP faces, now is the time to identify your unique ability to address these challenges. If you're like a high number of sales professionals, you may be struggling with identifying something that's unique to your product or service. It's understandable, given we live in a commoditized world. However, if you look deep enough, you can typically find an element to your product or service that really is unique. Keep in mind, uniqueness could also be represented in a combination of things that you do that no other competitor is able to accomplish.

Some examples of uniqueness in addressing the challenges of a sales leader could be training software that uses a unique spaced repetition approach to reinforce sales techniques. It could be software that takes data from the CRM, marketing database, and other sources of information to provide insights into the salesperson's behavior. Finally, it could be a custom playbook that increases conversion rates in the sales process.

If you are unable to identify something that is truly unique, then work with something that represents a strength. Specifically, identify the reason that you win more deals than not. That reason can be used in place of something that is truly unique. Obviously, you want to focus the conversation on a strength that has created success for you in the past.

Here's a great example. Several years ago, four major cellular carriers were launching the latest iPhone. Sprint and AT&T decided to run commercials that they hoped would cause consumers to sign up for their cellular service in conjunction with the latest iPhone. In these billion-dollar industries, any time they consider spending multiple millions of dollars on an ad campaign, obviously they want to focus on something that would cause the consumer to choose them. If they are going to spend millions of dollars in an ad campaign, they have to be sure the return in new customers is worth it. On the surface, it would look like the cellular industry is very commoditized and there would be nothing unique to showcase in the commercials. This was not the case.

Sprint at the time was the only cellular provider that had an unlimited data plan. So what they did was create a commercial that connected emotionally with the audience around the concept of being able to capture pictures, videos, and everything that's going on in an individual's life without having to worry about using up all their data. During the front part of the commercial, they're drawing on emotional videos and pictures while creating a compelling need or reason for the consumer to desire unlimited data. At the conclusion of the commercial, they make the statement, "Unlimited data—only with Sprint." This is a great example of a B2C company understanding the importance of building messaging around their uniqueness.

AT&T, on the other hand, took a different approach. In the beginning of the commercial, they show a kindergarten classroom and a teacher is having a conversation with three kids. At one point in the conversation, he asked if two is better than one. One of the kindergarten boys answers, "of course." The boy continued, "If you had one laser shooting out of your eye, you could blow up a bunch of things, but if you had two lasers coming out of both eyes, you could really blow things up."

They use this funny approach to spotlight that two is better than one. They then transition in the commercial to a statement that one can talk and surf at the same time. "Two is better than one. Only with AT&T."

This is a great example of both large carriers recognizing the need to identify something unique about a service that most people would view as commoditized. Once they identify the uniqueness, they then built the commercials to showcase or create a need or desire for the thing that is unique to them. Both of the commercials were making a statement that if you want this uniqueness in your life, you can only get it with them.

You have this same opportunity in how you speak about your product or service. This is the power of identifying something unique to your product or service in addressing the challenges of your prospects. There's power in being able to make the claim that if they want the outcome that you're discussing, the only place that they can get it is with you.

There's power in being able to make the claim that if they want the outcome that you're discussing, the only place that they can get it is with you.

You've read and now understand the building blocks that go into creating a value position. In order to understand how to create a value position statement, you need to understand the power of a single word that is the most engaging for your prospects.

This word first showed up back in the 80s in conjunction with direct mail campaigns. By the way, direct mail is making a comeback because email has become over-utilized.

The typical direct mail campaign would showcase the product or service that was being sold. For example, if a new gym is opening down the road, you'd receive a direct mail piece that would talk about their pool, racquetball courts, free weights, treadmills, and so on. Some people would respond to this approach and visit the gym.

However, what they discovered back in the 80s was if they introduced this word into the direct mail campaign, it would double the response rate. The word was "You."

You

Instead of the direct mail piece saying, "Come check us out, we have a pool, racquetball courts, etc." they wrote, "Imagine if *you* could have the body of your dreams. You can. Come check out our new gym." The second statement evokes the amygdala because you're talking about the prospect and their imagination by using the word *imagine*. This causes the prospect to start to imagine the outcome they desire, rather than focus on what the gym has to offer.

"You" vs. "we" vs. "I"

Obviously using "I" in a conversation creates too much focus on you instead of the prospect. As a salesperson, you've probably experienced or heard that you should find opportunities to use the word "we," but there's a challenge in using that word.

Imagine you've just gotten out of knee surgery and you're hitting the morphine pump for all it's worth. The surgeon walks in a couple hours after surgery and asks,

"How are we doing today?" The problem with the use of the word *we* is that the doctor is not experiencing the debilitating pain in your knee. They haven't earned the right to use "we."

The use of "we" can also be confusing. If you use "we" in a sales conversation, your prospect may be wondering if you are referring to "we," the company that you work for, or "we," you and them. Ultimately, it's confusing to try and figure out what you mean when you use the word "we." Or in some cases, you may use the word "we" when it's not appropriate like the example with the surgeon.

That leaves the word "you." Using "you" in the front part of a statement or question engages your prospect in a way that "I" and "we" never will. As soon as your prospect hears "you" in a conversation, it causes the prospect's amygdala to pay attention. Simply because the amygdala heard the word "you," anything that comes after that makes the amygdala want to know how the following information after "you" affects it.

You've already experienced the use of "you" in the reading of this book. As the author, I could have started the book by saying, "I'm going to describe;" or "I'm going to tell;" or "I'm going to show you something about a high-value conversation." Instead, I use the word "you": "You've already read;" "you're going to see;" "you're going to experience;" and so on. You should be able to start to feel the difference between the use of "I" and "you." The same is true for the contrast between the use of "we" and "you." "You" will always be the more engaging word to use in your conversations.

Unfortunately, changing the way that you speak and utilizing "you" instead of "I" or "we" is one of the most difficult transitions you'll make as a salesperson. The simple reason for this is that you have been hardwired to think about you: To look at the world and view it from your point of view. So it's only natural in the conversations you have that you would talk from your point of view and use the word "I."

In order to make the shift from using "I" to using "you," the first step is becoming aware of your use of "I" in a conversation. It's very similar to a public speaker who may use too many filler words. Words like "um," "so," and "and" can show up repeatedly when somebody first starts getting comfortable in public speaking. In order to reduce the amount of filler words, the first step that they must take is to become aware of their use. Once they are aware, then when they listen to themselves speak, they can identify when the filler words are showing up and effectively remove them from their speech pattern.

The same thing is true with the use of "you" instead of "I." Now that you are aware of your preference for using the word "I," when it shows up in your conversations with a prospect, you'll immediately hear it and start to change your speech pattern to using "you."

The use of "you" is prominent in the creation of a value position statement (VPS).

A value position statement is a statement of what your prospect can do differently as a result of your unique ability to solve a problem. To accomplish this, you cannot make any reference to your product or service in the statement. The statement will be created in a way that your prospect can start to imagine what their world would look like using your product or service.

A VPS will commonly start with, "imagine if you" or "what if you," followed by a statement of what they can do differently. Here are a couple of examples using the sales leader example earlier in this chapter.

Imagine if you could increase the number of reps on your team that are hitting quota.

What if you could onboard new reps so that they're hitting their revenue goal in six weeks instead of three months?

Imagine if you could sell a more diverse mix of products and services to expand your wallet inside of an existing account.

Notice that none of the previous VPSs made any reference to the solution. Let's address the obvious. The reference to value position *statements* can be confusing when they obviously are being constructed as a question. The reason behind the reference to them as a statement is that they're actually rhetorical questions. You'll read more later on the use of these VPSs in the context of a conversation and understand why they are rhetorical questions. By referring to them as statements, it helps to drive home the point that these aren't actual questions where you would pause and wait for the prospect to answer.

Up to this point, the focus has been on introducing the creation of a value position and a VPS for a sales leader from the perspective of a sales consultancy. Let's take a look at our example business, ERP Software Company, that recently went through this exercise.

ERP Software Company

ERP Software prides itself on being one of the first ERP solution providers to offer cloud ERP. Since 2007, ERP has delivered robust and reliable cloud-based ERP to a wide range of customers around the globe. Unlike many other ERP vendors, all ERP Software solutions are available in the cloud (also called Software as a Service, or SaaS) or as an on-premises installation.

In reading the above description of ERP Software Company, you've probably already noticed a couple of things that they're pointing out as different or unique.

ERP Software ICP

ERP Software's ideal customer persona is the owner or executive responsible for P&L in a manufacturing, distribution, or retail business with revenue of $2-to-$20 million that needs a solution for between five to twenty users. Obviously, the more specific your ICP, the easier to map your VPS and conversations to that persona.

Their primary objectives are:

1. Grow the business while maintaining accurate financial records.
2. Central platform that provides visibility into their business.
3. Deliver and provide high quality products and services.

Their primary challenges are:

1. Lack of meaningful operational insights like inventory, supplier performance, purchase order workflow, and end-to-end financials.
2. Time-consuming and complicated processes to get necessary business information out of disparate systems like QuickBooks and Excel spreadsheets or another ERP.
3. Costly consulting fees due to lack of flexibility and difficult-to-use existing software.
4. Inability to access the information on any device or platform, which leads to more inefficiency.

ERP Software's uniqueness is:

1. One integrated business management solution for all your growing business needs, ranging from finance to manufacturing to human resources and everything in between.
2. Availability on any device from laptops, tablets, and phones.

3. As the ERP leader in Europe, the software is fully developed, which translates into total cost of ownership up to 70% lower than comparable ERP systems (meaning ERP doesn't have to pass on development costs in a new market like the U.S.).

Identifying and documenting the information above to get to the elements that go into a value position is straightforward. You are the expert because you interact with different companies and prospects every day. In the months and years involved in building these relationships, you become more and more aware of what your prospect is trying to accomplish and what stands in their way.

Taking these building blocks and creating a VPS is a little more challenging, but worth the effort.

Before you read what goes into creating these VPSs, it's important to understand a crucial principle. It's a principle of impact.

You may remember a DIRECTV commercial that starts with an individual watching TV and his cable goes out. As the narrator for the commercial is describing the situation, the next statement that you hear is something like, "When your cable goes out, you get frustrated. When you get frustrated, you go to the gym to blow off steam. When you go to the gym to blow off steam, you play racquetball. When you play racquetball, you may get hit in the eye. When you get hit in the eye, you get an eye patch. When you get an eye patch, people want to know how tough you are. When people want to know how tough you are, you can end up in a roadside ditch. Don't end up in a roadside ditch. Get DIRECTV."

What you just experienced in that commercial is the principle of *impact*. This principle is that when you experience a challenge or a problem, that challenge or problem does not exist in isolation. For every challenge or problem that your prospects face, there's always an impact or a ripple effect that the problem creates inside of their business.

You're also going to see where this impact or ripple effect can show up in the creation of VPSs.

Let's see how this plays out for ERP Software. Below are example VPSs.

What if you could...

1. Run leaner, strengthen customer loyalty, and increase your bottom line?

2. Respond to market changes while increasing efficiencies in your operations?

3. Have freedom and peace of mind to focus on your company's growth and innovation?

These are the VPSs that ERP Software created. The way that they got here was to write the phrase, "What if you could...," and then come up with an answer that would describe what their prospect could do differently. Just like with challenges or problems having an impact inside of a business, value positions also create a ripple effect. In the example below, you'll see how ERP Software used this ripple effect to identify the best VPSs to use in their conversations.

To identify the impact or ripple effect for VPSs, you'll use the phrase, "So that you can." Here's what that looks like. Initially they answered the question, "What can the prospect do differently with...":

Having a holistic view of your business?

- So that you can run leaner.
- So that you can strengthen customer loyalty.
- So that you can increase your bottom line.

The principle used above is to write out what first comes to mind in what the prospect can do differently and right underneath put "so that you can..." and complete that statement. Once ERP Software exhausted all the "so that you can..." statements, they looked at them and decided the better VPS would be the following: *"What if you could run leaner, strengthen customer loyalty, and increase your bottom line?"*

If they had just stopped at, "have a holistic view of your business," they would have never come up with a more compelling VPS.

CHAPTER 4

CRAFT A
SALES CONVERSATION ROADMAP (SCR)

The Value Position Roadmap (VPR) allows you to incorporate the elements you identified in the previous chapter into a high value framework. The VPR will be utilized in the following chapters to build high value communication in prospecting and selling conversations.

road map (noun)

Definition of *road map* from *Merriam-Webster*
  a: *a detailed plan to guide progress toward a goal*
  b: *a detailed explanation*

This definition would aptly fit the book *Born to Run* by Christopher McDougall, which is a great example of a guide or detailed explanation that showed up in my life several years ago.

I started running when I was thirteen years old. I was sitting in the family room of our house, and my father walked in and challenged me to a race. I didn't necessarily want to get up from the couch and stop watching TV, but

I thought, Hey, he's an old guy. Should be pretty easy to beat him in a race.

So we put on our shoes and set off for a run with me having no idea of how far we were going to go. At about the mile and a half mark, my father looked at me and said, "I'll see you back at the house." I had this puzzled look on my face. What did he mean? He said, "The pace that we've been running is much slower than what I normally run, so I'm going to pick up the pace, and I'll see you back at the house." I was convinced that was not going to happen.

What I didn't take into consideration was that long distance running takes some practice in order to build up endurance. Sure enough, he finished about a quarter of a mile in front of me and was waiting back at the house. It was at that point I decided that he would never beat me in a foot race again. This launched my running career.

Over the years, I've logged enough miles to go completely around the equator, and after running all of those miles, I found that running had two primary benefits. The obvious one was the cardiovascular benefit, but the not-so-obvious one was this unique ability to solve problems.

If I have a challenge or problem in my personal or business life, I can hold that problem in my mind's eye and, as I'm running, the problem will work itself out. I find that I get creative ideas or thoughts much easier while I'm moving than while I'm sitting still. Running is something that is a part of who I am, and what I do is something that would be painful to give up.

Several years ago, my wife noticed when I would come in from a run that I would be limping. The limping comes from a knee injury I sustained playing soccer in my twenties. Over the years, my right knee and its cartilage have deteriorated to where running would cause bone on bone inflammation and arthritis. It had gotten to the point where I couldn't run the way that I've run over the years unless something changed.

I scheduled an appointment with an orthopedic surgeon who took x-rays of the knee and came back with what I suspected he would say: that it's time for a knee replacement. I realized that if I got a knee replacement, it would potentially be the end of my running career. This was a deal stopper for me.

About the same time that I went to go visit the orthopedic surgeon, a friend of mine recommended the book *Born to Run*. In the book, the author makes a case for running barefoot. As I was reading the book, I couldn't believe that running barefoot on concrete would actually be healthier for my knee. Having nothing to lose, I set out to learn how to run completely barefoot.

If you haven't read the book *Born to Run*, this may sound crazy that somebody with an arthritic knee can run eight miles barefoot. Here's why it makes sense.

Most people learn to run with a heel-strike rolling up onto the balls of their feet and continuing with that motion while they run. The reason that we run this way is because we have these massive, cushioned shoes on our feet. Running instructors will tell you a heel strike is actually counterproductive to the running because you're extending your leg and impeding your momentum.

Anytime that you encounter change, if you have the assistance of a road map, it minimizes the challenge of that change.

When you take your shoes off and run on concrete and plant your heel for a heel strike once, you'll never do it again. By being barefoot, the nerve endings in your feet will tell you the right form to run with. The correct form is to come down on the front or mid part of your foot and then land on your heel, keeping your feet underneath your body. By doing this, the impact of running is still mostly by your feet and your calf muscles. This is why in the book, McDougall suggest that you work up to your mileage over time. Your feet and calf muscles are not used to this type of form.

With most of the impact being absorbed by your feet and calf muscles, the impact is minimized for your knees, hips, and other joints (McDougall 2011). This is why I'm able to run completely barefoot for distances as long as eight miles.

So why the example of barefoot running? If I was going to continue to get the benefit of running, I was going to have to change the way I ran. Anytime that you encounter change, if you have the assistance of a road map, it minimizes the challenge of that change. You have the same opportunity when you look at changing the way that you conduct a conversation with a prospect by leaning into the sales conversation road map. Let's look at how to apply the road map with the information that you've already identified in the previous chapters.

The focal point of your conversations with your prospects should always be the value position and value position statement. These are what you want your prospects to remember after your conversation. But before you introduce the VPS in a conversation with a prospect, there are a couple of other steps that you need to take.

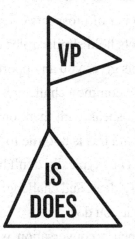

Value Positions are based on what your product is or
does uniquely to solve your "prospects" challenges.

Challenges

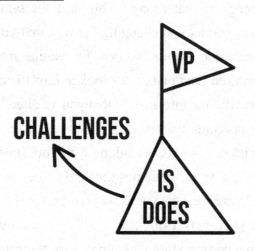

Challenges: Challenges you know your prospect faces.

As a sales professional you have the opportunity to speak with a large number of prospects every year. In most cases, these prospects hold similar roles or titles within their organization. This gives you an opportunity to understand some of the more common challenges that your prospects face because you speak with them on a daily and weekly basis. Keep in mind this is not true for the individuals that you speak with. They typically don't have the opportunity to share thoughts, ideas, and challenges with their peers in the same way that you do.

When you open a conversation with a prospect, you want to avoid playing twenty questions in the early part of the conversation. If you start a conversation with a question like, "What keeps you awake at night?", you're communicating to your prospect that you really don't understand their world. Additionally, the prospect gets frustrated because they're having to answer these types of questions any time they speak with a salesperson. This is not how you want to make a first impression with your prospects.

You have an opportunity to use the insights and understanding that you've gained in talking with similar prospects. The way to do this is to introduce known challenges that you've learned in working with your other prospects and customers. You also have an opportunity to introduce these challenges by saying, "In speaking with other prospects, we hear that they are challenged with..." and then fill in the blank. By doing this, you're not putting a finger on their forehead and saying they have these challenges, but you're also sharing challenges that you know they're experiencing because of the insights you have from other prospects.

Impact

Impact: The impact of those challenges in their business.

You've already read about the DIRECTV commercial where you can see the ripple effect of the cable TV going out. As a reminder, if cable TV goes out, the customer gets frustrated, and after walking through the consequences of that, he ends up in a roadside ditch. It's not enough to communicate the challenges that your prospect faces, but you also have the opportunity to speak to the impact that those challenges have on both the prospect and the company.

Consider the following example. An ERP company serves manufacturers and distributors and provides their software across any type of device that their customers would want to use. When they speak to their prospects, they uncover a typical challenge of the information that's used to run a manufacturer's business being stored in multiple locations.

Here's the impact. It takes too much time to access the necessary information to make decisions around inventory, materials, delivery, etc. This can lead to unacceptable customer service as far as delays and receiving what their customers have purchased. It could also have a negative financial impact if they don't have enough inventory or have too much inventory. If there's a negative financial impact, it could show up in missed revenue goals. Missed revenue goals could lead to missed payroll; missed payroll could lead to employees leaving; and then employees leaving could lead to the business having to close.

At this point, you can take what you've learned in previous chapters about challenges and the impact and plug them into the first part of the sales conversation road map. You looked at both the positive and negative of either using your service or product or not using your service or product. It should be fairly simple to go back and identify the ripple effect or impact that your prospect's challenges will have on their business. Make sure you pick their most damaging impact for the persona that you're speaking to during the sales process.

Do

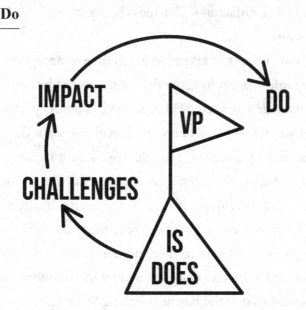

Do: What your prospect can do different with your unique ability
to solve their challenges.

Up to this point, you've successfully communicated to your prospect what their world looks like without your product or service. Now it's time to shift the conversation to what their world would look like with your product or service. This is where you introduce the value position statements that we discussed in chapter 3.

To continue the example of the ERP software provider, the value position statements look like this.

What if you could...

1. Run leaner, strengthen customer loyalty, and increase your bottom line?

2. Respond to market changes while increasing efficiencies in your operations?

3. Have freedom and peace of mind to focus on your company's growth and innovation?

After having successfully communicated that their challenge has an impact, you now flip the script to describe what their world would look like with your product or service. As a reminder, notice that the value position statements do not include any mention of a product or service. That comes later.

Proof

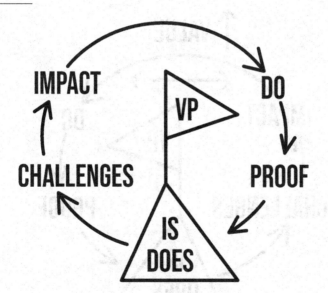

Proof: Case study or in software a demonstration.

At this point in the road map, you've successfully created a contrasting worldview so that the prospect can perceive the highest value. Now they want proof that what you've just communicated is real. It's as simple as identifying an existing client that would be the most relevant to the prospect you're speaking to. The simplest way to do this is to create a one-sentence case study.

Start with the problem, state what they were able to do differently, and conclude with how they solved the problem.

That's how XYZ manufacturer was able to overcome a lack of operational insights and increase efficiencies by using our ERP software.

Does

Now that you've successfully created a contrasting worldview for your prospect and provided proof, they will now want to know a little bit about how your product or service works. Specifically, what it does.

When creating this content, it's important to be clear and concise. The goal in using this road map is to communicate high value, offer some proof, and give a brief explanation of what your product or service does so that the prospect will want more information.

Impact of VPS, Credibility, Empathy, and Value

One of the most important things that you need to accomplish when talking to a prospect is to build credibility and trust. This potentially can be a challenge if your focus is slanted toward qualifying the prospect early in the relationship. In order to qualify, you have to ask a lot of questions. Asking a lot of questions early in the relationship can communicate to the prospect that you don't really understand their world.

By using the sales conversation road map and introducing known challenges and the impact of those challenges, you immediately build rapport, trust, and credibility with your prospect. They start to get a sense that you are a part of their tribe and understand the world that they live in. That's why it's important to start a conversation with the challenges and impact.

The goal in using this road map is to communicate high value, offer some proof, and give a brief explanation of what your product or service does so that the prospect will want more information.

When following the road map, you also successfully create a contrasting worldview which leads to our perception of high value. The result of using the road map is the ability to establish trust and credibility while communicating high value.

Example

Assume for a minute that you've never been exposed to a smartphone. You've lived the last twenty years blissfully unaware of the value or power of a smartphone.

You walk into a Verizon store one day, curious about what all this technology is about and ask the salesperson for the latest, greatest smartphone. When they find out that you've never experienced a smartphone, they'll immediately get excited and go grab the latest smartphone. At this point, they'll start communicating with you that it's made of gorilla glass, aluminum backing, 128 GB hard drive, 8-megapixel camera, and it weighs less than a pound. After sharing this with you, they immediately look at you and ask, "Don't you want one?"

Obviously if you've never heard of a smartphone, all that information at best would be very confusing, leaving you to still consider what's all the fuss about with smartphones. Now contrast that with this example.

You walk into an AT&T store and share the same information with the salesperson. Instead of bombarding you with techno jargon, they instead have been educated on how to use the sales conversation road map and carry a completely different conversation.

They start with asking questions about your life and specifically trying to get to areas where you have challenges personally that a smartphone could solve. So let's say that you share with the salesperson that you have a daughter and son-in-law who live completely across the country and have just given birth to your first grandchild. The salesperson then asks if that's frustrating or a challenge for you. The obvious answer is yes, you want to be with your daughter and son-in-law and to experience the wonder of having a grandchild. It leads to multiple flights across the country which can be expensive and, in some cases, the grandparents being separated because they can't travel together. With that in mind, the salesperson shifts the conversation from those challenges and starts to describe something different.

"What if you could see your grandchild every day just like he or she was standing right next to you? What if you could see their first steps? Maybe more importantly, what if you could see the expression on their face the first time they say 'Grandaddy'?"

"But you can. It's called a smartphone."

At this point, they would quickly demonstrate or prove the value by showing how you could use an app like FaceTime so your grandchild could see you and you could see them and experience what the salesperson just described.

You can quickly see that this is a completely different conversation than the first example where the salesperson just talked about what the smartphone was and what it does and didn't take the time to create this contrasting world to you.

Gong.io Validation

Gong.io is a software company that records sales conversations and is able to use artificial intelligence to provide insight around the effectiveness of the conversation. Having recorded thousands of sales calls and dissecting them from the standpoint of what works and what doesn't, they came to several conclusions.

Top-producing salespeople progress through their sales calls sequentially, not haphazardly.

Top-producing salespeople progress through their sales calls sequentially, not haphazardly. When you analyze the topics they discuss, they move from tone topic to a naturally-related topic.

The Sales Conversation Roadmap gives you a sequential framework leading to high perceived value.

CHAPTER 5

LEVERAGE THE POWER OF STORIES AND HOOKS

Stories and hooks are powerful tools to keep your prospects and customers engaged in your selling conversations.

One of my favorite places to run is on the beach of Fripp Island, South Carolina. Fripp Island holds a special place in my memories as I've vacationed there with my family, my kids, and my grandkids over the last 45 years.

A typical run at Fripp involves heading down to the beach and walking up some stairs over a platform to get you down to the beach. I typically run early in the morning before the sun is up, so I head in the direction of where the sun will be rising and start my run. Over the course of the next 30 to 45 minutes, I'll get to experience the sun coming up over the water and the stillness of a Fripp Island beach morning.

As you read the lines above, take a minute and identify: What color was the sand? How about the water? What did you see when I was describing the sun rising above the water? Was it red, orange, or what color did you perceive? The power of stories is that we draw from our own experiences to fill in the gaps and actively participate in the story that's being told. As humans, we don't experience a story passively; we experience stories actively.

Neuroscientist Uri Hasson researches the basis of human communication, and experiments from his lab reveal that even across different languages, our brains show similar activity or become "aligned" when we hear a story. This amazing neural mechanism allows us to transmit brain patterns, sharing memories and knowledge. "We can communicate because we have a common code that presents meaning," Hasson says.

During his TED Talk, he shows the brain patterns of two individuals before and during the telling of a story. Before the telling of a story, the brain patterns are separate for each individual. As soon as one of the individuals starts telling a story, the brain patterns become in sync or aligned. In his research, he discovered that there's no other type of medium like stories that can create this coupling between two individuals (Hasson 2016).

Stories have been used for thousands of years as a way for human beings to pass on information from one generation to the next. Because of the emotions involved in experiencing a story, we're able to remember the facts and information that are contextualized in a story. Stories can be used much like a trojan horse. In the telling of a story, you can contextualize important information for your prospects and customers that will make it easy for them to understand and remember the facts because they take place in the context of a story.

Personal Story

There are all types of stories you can use when communicating with others. In the business world, the most common stories are ones about our business experience. This makes sense because you're having business conversations.

Personal stories, for the most part, are not utilized in a business conversation because they seem out of place when the prospect or customer is expecting you to talk about business-related items. However, this dynamic actually makes personal stories more impactful. Going back to the success formula, one of the things you learned was introducing something unexpected into a conversation. Personal stories have that effect. When you start sharing a personal story, the person you're communicating with is wondering where you're going with that story because you are in a business setting.

Personal stories can have an amazing impact on your prospect as long as you tie the story to something that's important or relevant to them. Personal stories also have the effect of building rapport with your prospect because you're willing to share something personal about yourself.

Let's look at the steps that you can take to build a personal story. First thing to recognize is that because you need to land the story on something important or relevant to your prospect, you have to give some thought as to how to deliver the story before the conversation. It's one thing to open a conversation with talking about common interests like children, sports, or vacations, but it's another to use a personal story and tie it to something that's relevant to your prospect.

Here's an example of a personal story from a sales representative who worked for a telecommunications manufacturer called Mitel. The sales rep's name is Ken B. The opportunity that Ken was pursuing was with UPS. UPS had invited four competing companies to come in and pitch to an executive team for the executive team to choose two of the companies for a final round of presentations.

One of the best ways to use a personal story is in the opening of a meeting or presentation. Incorporating a personal story in the beginning of the meeting allows you to get comfortable in front of the room because you don't have to memorize anything. Ken opened his meeting this way:

"As I was driving over for the meeting today and thinking about the challenges that you face at UPS, it reminded me of my baseball career. I played as an All-Star pitcher at Georgia Tech and was drafted by the St. Louis Cardinals. Coming up through the ranks of minor league baseball, I was confronted with the reality that I could not hit a baseball. You may be thinking that's normal for a pitcher, but I couldn't hit a baseball as good as most pitchers.

"The reason that I couldn't hit a baseball is because there was too much inefficiency in my swing. When you're trying to hit a 95 mile per hour fastball and there's any unnecessary movement in your legs, hips, or arms as you swing across the plate, you'll never have an opportunity to hit the ball.

"At the time that I was playing baseball, there was a hitting coach who had video technology that could film at a very high frame rate. This allowed him to film me trying to hit a baseball and slow the video down enough to where he could show me the inefficiency in the different parts of my swing. By using the technology and combining it with his hitting acumen, I was able to improve my skill at hitting a baseball. As a matter of fact, the very first hit that I got was off Andy Pettitte at Triple-A while Andy was coming through the minor league ranks for the [New York] Yankees. I remember it like it happened yesterday.

"This is kind of like the challenge that you all face of driving inefficiency out of your voice and data networks. You need the combination of both technology and trusted advisors to combine your voice and data on a common platform and increase the efficiency of your network. Let's take a look at how that can happen by partnering with Mitel."

At this point, he moved to the next step in his presentation.

So, how does this example help you create your own personal stories? Let's look at what Ken did and unpack it in a way that will allow you to see how you can create personal stories in your selling conversations.

When creating a personal story, you have to start with the end in mind. Specifically, identify the challenge or what's at the heart of the challenge for your prospect. Then look back into your own life and find a story or a scenario where you faced a similar challenge. You then have the opportunity to tell the story and land on the thing that is relevant to your prospect or customer. This is exactly what Ken did while preparing for his meeting.

The reason that Mitel had invited these different companies to present to them was because of the inefficiency in their voice and data network. All Ken had to do was to find examples in his own life where inefficiency existed, how he was able to solve it, and then tie it to the situation that UPS was facing.

When telling a personal story, you need to keep a couple of things in mind. First, understand the audience you're communicating with. Use stories from your own life that your audience can relate to. Stay away from controversial topics like religion, politics, or—if you live in the Southeast U.S.—college football.

Second, keep the personal story to somewhere between four to six minutes. Anything shorter than that, and you really don't get the impact of telling a story. Anything longer than six minutes, and the intrigue you create by starting to tell a personal story will start to turn into frustration as your prospects try to figure out why you're telling the story.

Third, if you can find a personal story that paints you in a less than favorable light, use it. Coming across as vulnerable or transparent will cause your audience to respond in kind. No one likes to do business with somebody like Mary Poppins who is practically perfect in almost every way.

Finally, tell the story with the same emotion that you originally experienced it. If you tell a story from a factual standpoint and don't relive the emotion behind it as you're telling the story, your audience will never experience the emotion as well. If it's a frustrating story, let yourself relive the frustration. If it's a happy story, let yourself relive the happiness.

Personal stories can be used throughout your meetings or conversations. However, like some of the other techniques you've experienced in this book, you don't want to overuse any one of them, or the technique starts to lose its impact.

Overcoming Emotional Objections with Reframes

When speaking with a prospect, you can almost always expect some type of an objection. Objections come in two different forms. The first is a logical objection. This comes in the form of you not having a feature or capability associated with your product or service. The second is an emotional objection. This is when your prospect has a feeling or bias about your product or service. You should handle these two objections in completely different ways.

Logical objections should be handled logically. If your product or service does not have the capability that the prospect needs, you can spotlight or showcase other advantages that your product may possess.

However, for an emotional objection, a logical approach will not win the day. Basic human psychology says that you *cannot logic your way out of an emotional issue or objection*. You're dealing with two different parts of the brain. If a prospect has a bias or an emotional objection, it's rooted in the limbic system. If your prospect has a logical objection, it's rooted in the cerebral cortex. So when you try to overcome an emotional objection with a logical response, you're literally speaking in a way your prospect cannot relate to. They're speaking emotionally, and you're speaking logically.

One way to deal with an emotional objection is to use a reframe. Reframing is a technique used in therapy to help create a different way of looking at a situation, person, or relationship by changing its meaning. It helps one look at situations from a slightly different perspective.

The idea behind reframing is that a person's point-of-view depends on the frame it is viewed in. Think of a picture frame. If you have a picture hanging on a wall in your foyer or entryway that has been there for years, watch what happens when you take it down and put a new frame on it. The next time a friend or family member walks into your home to look at the picture, they comment, "Is that a new picture?"

The reason for this response is that the picture is viewed differently when you use a different frame. While reframing has been used in the therapy world, there's also an opportunity to apply this principle in dealing with your prospect's emotional objections. The way that you do this is by using a story, analogy, or metaphor that has nothing to do with the emotional issue of your prospect.

Here's a quick example that played out in a conversation between myself and my teenage daughter.

My daughter was fourteen going on twenty and came home from high school one afternoon and announced that she was going to a concert this weekend with some friends. When I pressed her as to where the concert was, she gave me a vague answer and finally told me that it was at a bar. However, this particular evening they would not be serving alcohol, they were just using the venue for a concert. When I pressed the reason more and asked how old the guys would be that were attending this concert, she said eighteen or nineteen years old. You're probably not surprised that my blanket response was no.

At this point, I could have taken two different approaches to support my decision of not allowing her to go to the concert. Obviously, she had a very strong emotional attachment to the idea of going to the concert. If I were to take the logical approach, I could explain to her that I had prepared for this moment in time as her father and had done some extensive research. The research is infallible and points to a less than successful life for fourteen-year-olds who go to concerts with eighteen-year-old men. If I presented this logical information to her, the response would be something like, "Shut up."

Again, you cannot logic your way out of an emotional issue. Go back to a conversation you had with a friend or family member about their fear of flying. That fear is rooted in the limbic system, and if you take a logical approach and communicate that based on research, it's safer to fly than it is to drive to the corner, you'll not get the result that you're looking for. The same is true in this situation.

I took a different approach. Without realizing what I was doing, I used a reframe. At the time this was going on, I was teaching my daughter how to drive. So I asked her where we went for the first couple of times that I put her behind the wheel of my car. Her response was the large parking lot at the Kroger shopping center down the road. I asked her why she thought that for her first time behind the wheel we were in the Kroger parking lot. At this point, she was getting defensive because she didn't know where the conversation was going. The silver standard response was, "I don't know."

I explained, "The reason that we're in the Kroger parking lot is that I want to see you demonstrate that you can make good decisions behind the wheel of a car in a safe environment. That way if you get confused or make a mistake, there's no risk of you damaging the car or a friendly bystander."

"So where do you think we'll go next?" I asked.

Again, the defiant response, "I don't know."

"We'll go to the neighborhood streets where it's a little more complicated so that again, you can prove that you make good decisions behind the wheel of a car. What if I were to put you in the passenger seat of my car and drive you down to I-285, pull off to the side of the road, then for the first time behind the wheel of the car ask you to drive me home from this eight-lane interstate?"

Her response: "No, that would be horrible and scary."

"That's kind of like what you're asking me to do in letting you go to a concert with eighteen- to twenty-year-old young men," I replied. "You've not proven to me that you can make safe social decisions in that type of environment. What I'm looking for, just like driving the car, is for you to prove to me that you can make safe social decisions in safer environments over time. As a matter of fact, by the time you hit thirty, you can date anybody you would like."

Her response: "Dad, I hate it when you make sense."

Using a story that had nothing to do with going to a concert allowed her to see the situation from a different perspective. From this new perspective, she was able to remove the emotion from the equation and see the reality of what she was asking me to do.

You have the same opportunity to use stories, analogies, and metaphors to help your prospects see their emotional objection in a different light. This gives them the opportunity to see things differently, apart from the emotion that they're feeling.

Reframes are one of the best techniques in addressing emotional objections. However, you don't want to try and create a reframe on the fly during a sales meeting. In order to deliver a reframe effectively, you need to prepare in advance. Here are the steps that you need to walk through to accomplish this.

The first step is to identify the most common emotional objections that you get in your selling conversations. Once you have identified an objection, you need to determine what's at the heart of the emotion or bias. For example, you may work for a company that is under twenty-five employees and you're actively selling to Fortune 2000 companies. From time to time, you may get the response, "I love everything that I've heard in our conversations, but I feel like you're too small for us to do business with."

Anytime you hear a prospect say, "I feel like" or "I believe" or "I think," whatever comes after that more than likely is going to be an emotional objection. In the example above, now that you know the root issue, you have the opportunity to identify a story, analogy, or metaphor that would paint being small in a positive light.

Here are some examples of when small would be good. Small enables you to be nimbler and respond to product or customer requests. Small enables you to provide more focus and attention to your customers. You can even give examples of how small has created great success, like when two men and a bicycle shop made flying possible.

Let's look at another example. You may get an objection where they say, "I feel like this is going to be too disruptive to our business." In essence, they're communicating that in order to realize the value of your product or service, they feel like it's going to be too disruptive or difficult for their business to adopt your technology. There may be some element of truth to this, but there is still opportunity to use a reframe.

Think of an example in your own life where you've experienced some disruption in order to gain the benefit of a new product or service. Think back to the early days of using an iPod or MP3 player. The disruption is that you have to digitize all your music and then figure out how to organize it and transfer it onto the MP3 player. If you have a rather large music collection, this could be very disruptive. However, in the long run, the value that you realized in experiencing a little bit of suffering far exceeds that momentary disruption. This is much like the emotional objection where your prospect feels like it would be too difficult to implement your solution.

You can incorporate any of the above themes into a story or just use it as a quick analogy. Here's an example of a process that you can use to incorporate a story or analogy in the form of a reframe.

Always start by rephrasing the objection that you just heard from the prospect. You can say, "So what I hear you saying is that it would be too disruptive to implement our solution." Wait for the prospect to respond with a yes or no to provide further clarification. Once you understand and are clear about the emotional objection, you can introduce a reframe by saying something like, "That sounds a lot like…"

After you've shared the analogy or story that allows them to see their emotional objection in a positive light, you can then transition into more of a logical response to the objection. It's important to note that the reframe must come first so that they can see their objection in a positive light before you introduce a logical response to their objection.

So after delivering the reframe, you can then transition into a logical response like, "As a matter of fact, XYZ company had the same concern, and as it turned out, it only took three weeks for them to implement our solution." A year later you would have a hard time getting them to agree that the momentary pain had not been worthwhile.

At this point, you can ask again, "What do you think?" Hopefully they'll say something along the lines of, "I never looked at it that way. Let's continue the conversation."

Here's how you would pull this all together for the objection of your product or service being too disruptive for them to implement.

"If I understand you correctly, you feel like our product or service would be too disruptive to your business to implement?" They respond with a yes.

"That's interesting. It sounds a lot like the push back that people had when thinking about moving from CDs and cassette tapes to MP3 players. In the early days of this technology, if you wanted to take advantage of an MP3 player, you had to first digitize your music and then find a way to transfer it to the MP3 player. Depending on the size of your music library, this could take hours or even days to accomplish. However, for these early adopters, once they had all their music on a single device that allowed them to listen to it whenever and wherever they happened to be, they would tell you that they would never go back to the old way of consuming music.

"This is a lot like the situation you're facing with your business. In order to realize the long-term benefit and value of a product or service, it will require some changes and some momentary distraction to your business. However, what most of our clients have experienced is that in the long run they would never go back to the situation that they were in before.

"As a matter of fact, ABC company was concerned about the very same thing. A year and a half later, they would never consider going back to the old way of doing things. Additionally, if you'd like to speak with one of the principals of this business, we can arrange for that conversation.

"So now what do you think?"

Using a reframe is the right way to respond to an emotional objection, but it's not a silver bullet to get them to agree to move forward. It gives them the best opportunity to see the truth about the objection that they've given you. You have the opportunity to keep track of the emotional objections or biases that your prospects feel about your product or service and over time create a number of reframes that you can use in your selling conversations.

Customer Story

A customer story or a case study is a very common way to build credibility in the eyes of your prospective client. It provides a foundation for them to understand that companies have gone before them and have successfully realized the value of your product or service. However, there's an opportunity to integrate the principle of creating a contrasting worldview into the case study so that your prospect can perceive high value in the context of a customer story.

The way to accomplish this is pretty straightforward. Simply describe what the world of your client looks like before implementing your product or service. In addition to identifying the challenge and impact, provide some numbers around key performance indexes (KPIs) that accurately describe the pain of their situation before implementing your solution.

Then transition into describing what the world would look like today with your product or service. If you included numbers that reflected their current state in the form of KPIs, you now have the opportunity to contrast the former numbers with the new KPIs that resulted from the implementation of your solution.

Number Story

You've already read the importance of creating intrigue or doing something unexpected in your selling conversations to ensure that your prospects are paying attention and remember the most important things you're communicating. One of the ways to do that is through the use of a number story.

This technique involves introducing three numbers into the conversation. You can do this using a standing flip chart, a whiteboard, or by using a PowerPoint slide that builds with the three numbers. You introduce the three numbers by saying, "There's an interesting story about these three numbers." You can also use a phrase like, "There's a disturbing story" or "an intriguing story" or "an insightful story," depending on the story that the numbers are tied to.

Once the three numbers are in view, you then deliver the story that is tied to the three numbers. In some cases, you may want to convey information about the business that you represent instead of talking about the number of years you've been in business, the number of customers that you serve, or some other metric.

You can use this approach in a number of ways to introduce meaningful information for your prospect or customer. Find credible third-party information that your prospect may not be aware of. Typical sources can be with Forester, Gartner, or any research organization that is affiliated with the market that you serve.

You can also use numbers to paint a picture of your prospect's current state by drawing from average KPIs that may exist in their industry. There's a lot of creativity that can be used with this technique. Just make sure that you don't overuse it. Typically, once or twice in a meeting is more than enough.

Here is another example where credible third-party data is used to paint a picture and make a point that's relevant to your world.

"There's a disturbing story around these three numbers: 270, 500, 350. It's never been more difficult to get people's attention than it is today. There are over 270 billion emails, 500 million Facebook posts, and 350 million tweets sent every day. What this means is that your ability to be relevant and memorable in your sales conversations has never been more important than it is today."

CHAPTER 6

PROSPECTING TO WIN USING SCR

In this chapter, you will learn how to use the Sales Conversation Road Map (SCR) to get your prospects' attention to schedule an appointment or call.

To accomplish this, we'll cover:

1. Noise, attention, relevance?
2. LinkedIn profile
3. Emails
4. Cold calls
5. One-sentence case study
6. Exercise

Let's continue with the number story from the end of chapter 5 here to begin looking at the SCR.

There's a disturbing story around these three numbers: 270, 500, 350. There are over 270 billion emails, 500 million Facebook posts, and 350 million tweets sent every day. This doesn't include the fact that everyone carries a device called a smartphone that's constantly vying for their attention. It's never been more difficult to get people's attention than it is today.

Let's look at some of the different ways sales professionals have prospected over the years.

If you want to go way back in time, some of the more prevalent means for prospecting or getting customers' attention can be traced back to radio and TV. Or if you're old enough, maybe you remember the early Sears catalogs. There were also the door-to-door salesmen, who made the rounds to homes and/or offices.

With all the different mediums at your disposal, one would think that prospecting would become easier. Actually, it's just the opposite. With so many mediums to choose from, it becomes difficult to leverage all of them effectively.

As long as the telephone has been around, so has cold calling. This was a much simpler means for getting your prospects' attention or scheduling an appointment. All you had to do was pick up the phone and call the interested party, deliver a succinct value message, and schedule an appointment. In today's world, more and more businesses are doing away with office phones and having their employees use their cellphones. This obviously makes it more challenging to get to your prospect via the phone.

Direct mail came on the scene in the late 60s and early 70s and saw its heyday in the 80s. Then with the advent of the internet, everyone started building their websites. Not too long after that, email became the primary medium for prospecting along with cold calling.

As the internet started to evolve, we then saw the introduction of social media. Everyone was trying to figure out how to use Facebook, blogs, Instagram, LinkedIn, and other social media platforms. With all the different mediums at your disposal, one would think that prospecting would become easier. Actually, it's just the opposite. With so many mediums to choose from, it becomes difficult to leverage all of them effectively.

What this means is that your ability to be relevant and memorable in your sales communications has never been more important than it is today. Let's take a look at how you can do this with some of the more common communication mediums.

LinkedIn Profile

LinkedIn is a business and employment-oriented service that operates via websites and mobile apps. Founded on December 28, 2002 and launched on May 5, 2003, it is mainly used for professional networking, including employers posting jobs and job seekers posting their CVs. As of 2015, most of the company's revenue came from selling access to information about its members to recruiters and sales professionals. Since December 2016, it has been a wholly-owned subsidiary of Microsoft. As of June 2019, LinkedIn had 630 million registered members in 200 countries.

With over 630 million registered members, this obviously represents a fertile ground for prospecting. The interesting thing is that 95% of the 630 million users still use LinkedIn as an online resume ("LinkedIn" n.d.). This is fine if you're wanting to share your experiences and skill sets with recruiters who potentially would contact you for a job opportunity. However, if you'd like to utilize LinkedIn from a prospecting perspective, prospects don't care about your skills or previous experience. What prospects care about are the challenges they face and your ability to potentially solve those problems.

The fact that most LinkedIn users utilize it for employment networking means there's an opportunity for you to stand out. You have the opportunity to update the information about yourself so that it's more relevant to the prospects you hope to engage. To accomplish this, you need to change the content associated with your profile. Specifically, the headline and the "About" section of your profile.

When looking to change your headline, think in terms of a marketing tagline. What you want to communicate in the headline is succinctly stated in the outcome that you create or deliver for your clients. Let's use the ERP software provider referenced in chapter 3 as an example.

If you remember, the ICP for the ERP Software Company was the manufacturing business owner or operations manager. In creating a headline, you can include the title of the persona you wish to engage. Then you create a succinct statement of what that individual can do as a result of using your product or service. The easiest way to get to this headline would be a combination of the value position statements that you created back in chapter 3. For the manufacturing business owner, it would read something like this: "We help manufacturing business owners grow their business through efficiencies created by timely insights."

In addition to addressing your ideal persona and stating outcomes that they can realize by using your product or service, it's also important to create intrigue. Intrigue leads to curiosity, and curiosity leads to a prospect wanting to learn more about how you create the outcome stated in the headline. You should also use your headline as a tagline for any posts or messages that you send inside of LinkedIn. This creates a branding effect where your prospects see the headline again and again.

The next section that you'll want to update in LinkedIn is in the "About" portion of your profile. Again, most individuals using LinkedIn include a job summary of their responsibilities, goals, and achievements. This information is important to a potential recruiter but is mostly useless to the prospects you hope to engage. Keep in mind that this content in the "About" section can be changed and updated whenever you like. If you find the need to use your LinkedIn profile more from a job-search standpoint, you can always go back and change this content.

The "About" section can be built using the SCR introduced in chapter 4. You start with the challenges and expand on the impact of those challenges, paint a picture of what they can do differently, provide a little bit of proof, and then give a call to action. You've already read on how to identify this content in previous chapters. Now all you need to do is repurpose your profile in LinkedIn.

Before looking at an example of the "About" section, using the information from the ERP Software Company, look at a typical example found on LinkedIn for an ERP sales executive.

Headline:

Enterprise Software Sales Executive

About:

Enterprise Software Sales Executive with a track record of exceeding expectations. Experienced in commercial accounts as well as government/military contracts. I am well-versed in all phases of delivery for complex technologies.

With technical knowledge across enterprise software, semiconductors, telecommunications, and capital equipment, I have proven my ability to master the latest technologies and efficiently develop solutions for clients. With solid field training in high-activity transactions, I know how to build a balanced pipeline and close deals. Through process improvements and leveraging different marketing strategies, I have expanded market share and increased profits in the toughest of territories. I have proven my ability to create demand from scratch, as well as to cross-sell training and consulting services.

My career hallmark is that I have repeatedly been recruited to manage strategic customers. I am well-versed in collaborating with globally dispersed teams to deliver products that help clients make smart, timely business decisions and achieve new levels of productivity. I am trusted with big deployments because I know how to manage the ecosystem of overlays. I know the pain points of my customers and how to consult to bring products to market that will integrate across the value chain.

The above content is appropriate for someone who is looking for their next career move. But for any prospect for the sales executive, the content in their LinkedIn profile is never going to resonate in a way that causes the prospect to engage this person in a conversation.

Contrast this content below with the content for the "About" section for the ERP company.

Headline:

Equipping Manufacturing Executives with timely insights they need to profitably grow their business.

About:

As the lead executive for a manufacturing business, change is constant. Not just the changing competitive landscape, but change inside your business.

Change happens daily in inventory, supplier performance, and purchase order workflow. What doesn't change is the challenge of keeping up with this data. Not just keeping up but being able to extract insights from this data.

As we talk with your peers, we hear that this challenge becomes even more painful as the information needed to run the business lives in different databases. Financials are in QuickBooks, but the other information lives in spreadsheets or an existing ERP system. Getting these systems synced or talking to each other is time consuming and can lead to costly consulting fees.

What this means is an inability to provide the best customer service and compete and win in your market. With that as a backdrop, what if you could:

- *Grow the business while maintaining accurate financial records.*
- *Access a central platform that provides visibility into their business.*
- *Deliver and provide high quality products and services.*

You can, by using XYZ ERP software.

ERP software provides on integrated business management solution for all your growing business needs. You can access this information on any device since the software and its data lives in the cloud. As the ERP leader in Europe, the software is fully developed, which translates into total cost of ownership up to 70% lower than comparable ERP systems in the U.S.

If you need to make quick business decisions and gain easy access to the insights that drive these decisions, reach out to us here on LinkedIn or by email at john.doe@erpsoftwareus.com.

You can quickly see the difference between the two profiles. You only have a few seconds to make an impression on potential prospects when viewing your profile on LinkedIn. It's on you to make sure the content in your profile is as relevant as possible for your prospect.

Emails

As mentioned previously, 270 billion emails a day is a lot of noise to cut through in trying to get the attention of your ideal prospect. There has been a lot written about an effective prospecting email. You'll find a recap in the information below. However, the primary focus will be on how to use the value position road map to create relevant and insightful content in the body of the email.

The most important part of an effective prospecting email is the subject line. It's the first impression you make with your prospect. The most effective subject lines will be relevant and evoke curiosity and intrigue in your prospect.

According to a 2022 blog article created by the VP of Sales at Outreach, Mark Kosoglow, here are the five elements that need to go into an effective subject line.

1. They're short, sweet, and straight to the point.

2. They're written in a human way—non-formatted, casual subject lines seem more personal.
3. They're personal—they directly reference the company or the prospect's name.
4. They include a simple call to action.
5. They're relevant to the role, title, and persona of who we are reaching out to.

Here are some examples of subject lines from the same post (Kosoglow 2022):

Subject 1: The Connect Request

What to say: "Connect?"

Results: 52% open rate

Why it works: It's concise, purposeful, and matter of fact—the call to action is a simple and quick "yes" or "no" answer. But it's also ambiguous enough to create a sense of curiosity. We're wired to be curious—so much so that the reward centers in our brain light up whenever our curiosity is piqued. This approach makes your recipient want to know more (Connect about what? And why?) and open your email...

Subject 2: The Statistics

What to say: "6.8 people involved in a decision"

Results: 68% open rate

Why it works: People like numbers. Numbers stand out like an island in the sea of text saturating your prospect's inbox. They convey value, and if they have a decimal point, they seem more accurate and trustworthy. A hard statistic is built on more than just a seller's personal interpretation...

Subject 3: The Humble Ask

What to say: "Any response would be appreciated"

Results: 65% open rate

Why it works: Controversial rule of thumb: if it costs them little, most people want to help. We spend all day, every day trying to be of service to the people around us—our employers, our coworkers, our friends, and families. That drive can be habit-forming, and the request for "any response" conveys the idea that a simple "Yes," "No," or "You should talk to (this person)" will suffice.

Subject 4: #NoShame

What to say: "Shameless last attempt"

Results: 63% open rate

Why it works: This kind of candor is breaking a pattern. We're wired to have our curiosity piqued by this kind of exception to the rule. This subject line brings up an interesting caveat though—what works in your sales messaging is always a moving target. This 63% figure holds true over the three years we've tracked it, but as these "breakup" messages have become more common, they've also become more polarizing. Polarizing can be good, but this is something to keep an eye on. This is something to remember when reading any blog post like this one: what works today might not work in a year.

Again, these are just a few examples of how to create a compelling subject line. You can find many more. I simply Googled effective subject lines for prospecting.

Body

By now you're familiar with the story arc of the sales conversation road map. Just like other forms of communication, you want to create intrigue and communicate value so that the recipient will engage with you in a conversation. The structure is very similar to the content in the "About" section of the LinkedIn profile you read earlier. Look at how it's edited to be more concise in the form of an email.

Lead with something that is eye opening, credible, and challenges the status quo of the business.

> *Having worked in the manufacturing industry for years, I thought you'd find this interesting.*

> *85% of small to mid-sized manufacturers are losing up to 5% in margin due to an inability to manage and track critical business data (according to lead analysts in the manufacturing industry). This is compounded by the pace of change in the industry.*

Tie this credible piece of information to their business.

Change happens daily in inventory, supplier performance, and purchase order workflow. What doesn't change is the challenge of keeping up with this data. Not just keeping up but being able to extract insights from this data.

Describe how this plays out in their world.

As we talk with your peers like [name drop existing client], we hear that this challenge becomes even more painful as the information needed to run the business lives in different databases. Financials are in QuickBooks, but the other information lives in spreadsheets or an existing ERP system. Getting these systems synced or talking to each other is time consuming and can lead to costly consulting fees.

What's the impact?

What this means is an inability to provide the best customer service and compete and win in your market.

Paint a picture of a better world by describing what they can do differently with your solution.

With that as a backdrop, what if you could:

- *Grow the business while maintaining accurate financial records.*

- *Access a central platform that provides visibility into their business.*
- *Deliver and provide high quality products and services.*

Give them a brief description of how you create this better world for them.

You can, by using XYZ ERP software.

ERP software provides on integrated business management solution for all your growing business needs. You can access this information on any device since the software and its data lives in the cloud. As the ERP leader in Europe, the software is fully developed, which translates into total cost of ownership up to 70% lower than comparable ERP systems in the U.S.

Call to action.

If you need to make quick business decisions and gain easy access to the insights that drive these decisions, let me know when we can schedule twenty minutes to discuss.

Cold Calls and Outbound Prospecting

Call reluctance is something that every sales professional deals with at some point in their career. Asking several hundred sales professionals why this is, the most common response is they don't like interrupting someone else's day with an unexpected call. We've all experienced it. We're in the middle of something, the phone rings, and we decide even though we don't recognize the caller to answer the phone, only to hear the beginning of some sales pitch. That's the problem. Nobody is waiting by their phone for your call to sell them something. They are, however, interested in your ability to solve a problem.

Before you look at the right way to message a cold call, it's important to look at the emotional aspect of cold calling. How you "feel" about it will have a direct impact on your results.

I remember a conversation with a business development representative at a networking event. It went something like this. What company do you work for? *I work for a data warehouse.* What is your role in the sales organization? *I'm a business development representative.* So, you make a lot of outbound cold calls? *Yes, that's correct.* How's it going? *Not so well; it's uncomfortable making the calls knowing that I'm interrupting people's days. I understand as I've been on the receiving end of a lot of cold calls.*

Let me ask you a different question. How are your customers better off as a result of utilizing your services? Give me an answer without saying anything about the data warehouse. He looked at me a little puzzled but replied with, *Peace of mind.* When I asked why, he replied that the level of security and protection they provide gives their customers a sense of confidence that their data is well protected. I asked what else? He answered, *time savings*. When I asked why, he replied the work that they were doing internal to their business as it related to managing their data they are no longer responsible for. This means they can spend more time on things that will have a bigger impact on their business.

With this new information, I then asked, so with the world that we live in today where most people have little time and more anxiety, do you have a hard time picking up the phone and introducing peace and time freedom? He looked at me and replied, *I never looked at it that way*.

This is common for most salespeople when prospecting. They're thinking about it the wrong way. They're not calling to introduce a product or service; they're calling to introduce the outcomes that they create for their prospects. Once this business development representative realized how he could positively impact another human being, it made a world of difference in his ability to pick up the phone and make these calls.

Below you'll find a sample outbound cold call script that you can modify for your product or service. The goal of this call is to simply get the prospect to agree to a time end date for the discovery call. The goal is not to go into detail about the product or service if and when you get somebody to answer the phone. In the example below, you'll see a couple of principles used in outbound calling.

First, go ahead and acknowledge that you're interrupting their day. This helps diffuse the awkwardness of speaking to someone that's not expecting your call. Second, you'll want to state the purpose of the call which is to schedule a time where you can go into more detail about the benefit that you're going to introduce in your prospecting call. Third, keep the focus of this brief interaction on the main goal which is to get a time and date for a discovery call. If the prospect asks what this is about, simply refer back to the goal of setting that time and date where you can have a conversation with them about the benefit associated with your product or service.

Outbound Cold Call Script

Hi, this is [your name] from ERP Software, I know I'm an interruption; may I have "27" seconds to tell you why I called?"

Yes, continue.

No, when would be a better time to cover that 27 seconds.

XYZ ERP software has helped other manufacturers grow their business while maintaining accurate financial records, delivering a central platform that provides visibility into their business, and providing high quality products and services to their clients.

As the ERP leader in Europe, the software is fully developed, which translates into total cost of ownership up to 70% lower than comparable ERP systems in the U.S.

The reason I reached out to you today is to get a spot on your calendar to share how you can experience the same results in your business.

Would you have 20 minutes this Wednesday or Friday at 10 a.m.?

Get their name/email, and the person that manages the relationship with the agency.

CHAPTER 7

POSITION THE FIRST SELLING CONVERSATION FOR THE WIN

Next you will learn how to use the Sales Conversation Road Map (SCR) to communicate high value for your product or service in the first meaningful conversation with a prospect.

Why vs. Means

You read in chapter 3 about Simon Sinek and his book, *Start with Why*. The takeaway is that the most successful businesses are very clear about why they exist. You also read that there's a similar principle in successful sales conversations. A successful sales conversation will lead the prospect to understand what your product or service means to them. When they understand the meaning, they'll be interested to learn how your product or service works.

This first meaningful conversation or discovery call should be constructed in a way where the meaning is very clear to the individual you're speaking with.

First Impressions

You spent all this time and effort to earn the opportunity to speak with a prospect about the product or services that you represent. This initial conversation is the most important conversation in your relationship with the prospect. If this conversation does not go well, there is no second.

There are four objectives that you need to accomplish in this first conversation in order to make a great impression.

Rapport

Building rapport is all about finding and communicating common ground that you have with a prospect. It could be living in the same part of the country, individuals that are common to your network, or a common connection around sports. It's all about identifying common interests and introducing those into the conversation up front.

This initial conversation is the most important conversation in your relationship with the prospect. If this conversation does not go well, there is no second.

You should also pay attention to the tone that you bring to the conversation. Your voice should be positive, energetic, and upbeat. As you're breaking the ice with your prospect and developing rapport in the early part of the conversation, keep the topics that you introduce positive. Stay away from making comments about nasty weather, traffic, negative news—any of these topics will set the wrong tone for the rest of the conversation. Even if the negativity has nothing to do with you, the negative topic will be associated to you. This is not what you want in the opening of a conversation with a stranger.

Credibility

Historically, sales professionals have been trained to uncover needs and challenges of their prospect early in the conversation. This can often take the form of something that feels like twenty questions to the prospect. Using this approach can sometimes make the prospect feel like they're involved in an interrogation, but the more damaging aspect of playing twenty questions is that you're communicating to the prospect that you really don't understand their world. In today's world where we have access to all kinds of information via the internet, there's no excuse for not having some context and background about your prospect.

Credibility is established two different ways: early in the conversation and over time. To establish credibility early in the conversation, it's important to do some research and use what you already know about the market and role of the person you'll be meeting with. Most sales professionals build relationships with the same persona inside the business. Having numerous conversations with these individuals, over time you should develop a deep understanding of what they're trying to accomplish in the typical challenges that they face. By introducing these early in the conversation, your prospect starts to get a sense that you really understand their world.

Trust

Unfortunately, trust is something that really is established over time. It's a combination of realistic commitments and your ability to meet those commitments over time. When you do this, trust is established.

Meaning/Value

You've already read in previous chapters the importance of communicating high value to your prospect. In this initial conversation, it's up to you paint a picture of what their world looks like without your product or service and contrast that with what their world could look like with your product or service. When you do this well, your prospect will want to understand how you're able to create this world with your product. This interest in understanding *how* will ensure you get an opportunity to prove or demonstrate the value of your product in a second meeting.

I Don't Understand What You Do

When speaking with a prospect for the first time, you obviously would not want them to say to you, "I still don't understand what you do," toward the end of the conversation. Working with hundreds of sales professionals, I've had the opportunity to review hundreds of calls. Typically, I'll do this in advance of a consulting engagement to get a sense of how effective the sales team members are in their first meaningful conversation with a prospect.

Obviously, the most important conversation in any selling relationship is the first one. If this conversation is not conducted in a way that communicates high value and meaning to the prospect, the likelihood that you'll get another opportunity to speak with them will be low. This reality became painfully apparent for me while reviewing the first conversations for a software company in Atlanta.

> *Obviously, the most important conversation in any selling relationship is the first one. If this conversation is not conducted in a way that communicates high value and meaning to the prospect, the likelihood that you'll get another opportunity to speak with them will be low.*

In my initial conversation with the sales leader, he shared with me that they were only converting about 8% of their first conversations into the next stage of the sales process. This problem was even more painful for the sales leader as he was paying about $250,000 a year to outsource the business development function in creating first conversations for his sales team. With an 8% conversion rate, he was not able to justify continuing to use this business development company.

I asked the sales leader for five to ten recordings of the initial conversations that his sales team was having with their prospects. The sales team members were highly tenured and highly compensated, so I was surprised at how ineffective they were in these initial conversations. The common mistake that showed up in just about every call was a focus on what their software did and not so much on the problems that they solved. To make matters worse, the explanation of what they did was often confusing, and that is what ultimately led to a prospect making the statement, "I don't understand what you do."

After interviewing a number of team members inside the software company and speaking with some of their clients, we created a framework and a suggested script for the first conversation. This included the application of the sales conversation road map in constructing a conversation through which we communicate high perceived value to their prospects. After reviewing the draft of the initial conversation with the sales leader, we took the sales team through a training exercise and role played on how to use the framework. Each team member had to certify with the sales leader that they could effectively conduct a call using the sales conversation road map.

Checking back in almost four months later, I learned that after certifying the team on the use of the sales conversation road map, the following quarter their conversion rate for that first call went from 8% to 47%, more than six times the original conversion rate on their first calls, hence why this book is titled "6X—Convert More Prospects to Customers."

You might assume that the goal of your first meaningful conversation with a prospect is to educate them about your product or service. You would be mistaken. The goal is tied to what you learned in chapter 2 in the diagram where you read about understanding your product from the perspective of what it means, what it does, and what it is. The goal of the first conversation is to communicate high value and meaning to the individual you're conversing with.

Every meaningful conversation starts with understanding the world of the person you're speaking to.

Introduction

In this first meaningful conversation with a prospect, it's important to make the right impression. To accomplish this, you should open your introduction with a clear outline for the call. This would include the following:

- The meeting's purpose
- The buyer's agenda and expectations
- The amount of time set aside for the meeting
- The meeting's intended outcome
- Building rapport

In a real sales call, that might sound like this:

"The purpose of this call is to discuss how you can [avoid the pain of their current state] and achieve [outcome of the value position statement]."

"By the end of this call, you'll be in a position where you're either interested in these outcomes and we plan the next step; or if you're not interested, you tell me that, and we avoid wasting your time."

"Now to achieve that, we have thirty minutes set aside. Does that still work for you?

"Great. You'll hear all about A, B, and C. Is there anything else you'd like to cover?"

"Sounds good! Let's get started."

"I noticed on your LinkedIn profile that you [summarize their role and experience], can you expand on that?"

Challenges

You've already learned that in order for your prospects and customers to perceive high value for your product or service, the benefits you provide have to be contrasted with the challenges they experience currently. Too often, sales professionals focus too much on benefits and outcomes without addressing the prospect's status quo.

As a sales professional you speak with more companies and prospects than your customers. Your customers only know what's going on inside of their business and don't have the opportunity that you have to network and speak with other professionals in similar positions. This is why early in the conversation with the prospect, you don't want to ask questions about their challenges. This only communicates to them that you don't really understand their world.

Instead, take advantage of the fact that you get to speak with more professionals and learn about the specific and unique challenges that they face.

In this section of the discovery call, you want to introduce the things that you've learned from other prospects and customers to your prospect. It will sound something like this.

"In speaking with other professionals like you, we hear that they're trying to [insert goal or objective for this particular individual], but they're challenged with [insert two to three challenges that you know that they face that your product or service can solve]."

By using a third-party reference, in speaking with other professionals, you avoid making an assumption that they're experiencing these exact challenges. However, in most cases as you're describing what other professionals are dealing with, your prospect will be living in those challenges themselves.

For value to resonate, you must sell buyers on a problem (i.e., get them to admit to it). The best way to achieve that is to invoke self-discovery. By summarizing challenges you know they face, you get the buyer to self-identify with the problem your solution solves.

If you can get your buyer to *see* themselves in a story, they will come to their own self-discovery about the problem.

Which leads us to one of the best questions you can ask a prospect after introducing the challenges. A question that automatically gets them to *see themselves* in the story.

Impact/Qualify

You've just introduced the challenges you know they face. Now ask this question: "These are the challenges we're hearing from your peers; I'm curious, what do these look like in your world?"

By asking this question, you give the prospect an opportunity to visualize and remember how these challenges impact their world. Again, it gives them the opportunity to live in the story. The other reason for asking what it looks like instead of what it feels like is because the way humans remember is by conjuring up images and the associated feelings. So not only will a prospect visualize the problem, but they'll also experience the emotion associated with it.

The question is also a great example of a good open-ended question. You want to avoid asking closed-ended questions during discovery like, "Are you experiencing these problems?" This is a typical yes or no question. If they answer *no*, where do you go in the conversation? If they answer *yes*, you don't really learn much more than just a simple yes. The purpose of discovery is to learn as much as you can about the prospect's world.

A typical response to this question will be, "Yes, I'm experiencing some of those challenges, but I'm also dealing with these problems." As they share more about their world and the challenges that they face, you have an opportunity to accomplish two important things in this discovery call.

First, to deepen the perceived pain around their current state. You can accomplish this by asking impact questions. How are these challenges impacting your team? What is the impact on your ability to serve your clients? What's the impact on the business? What happens if you can't solve these problems?

All these questions invite the prospect to live in the conversation in a way that they experience the pain associated with their status quo. One cautionary note. A typical discovery call will not last more than about thirty minutes. If you ask too many impact questions, your prospect will get frustrated and want you to move on because they're still wanting to hear more about how you can solve their problems. You'll know that you've asked enough questions at this stage of the discovery call when they start giving you one- or two-word answers and the tone of their voice shifts.

The second thing that you need to accomplish at this point in the conversation is to qualify the prospect. You need to ask questions in order to determine if they are really a good fit for your product or service.

However, qualifying questions that show up earlier in the conversation can make the prospect feel like you're just trying to qualify them instead of really build rapport and a relationship with them.

I can remember experiencing this as I was speaking to the CEO of a software company. We were exploring a partnership opportunity. Not more than two minutes into the conversation, he was asking questions around my typical clients—their size, industry, and revenue—and specific names of companies. I made a decision to end the conversation, feeling like this was not going to be a productive partnership, but they were merely looking for a couple quick hits by partnering and having access to my customer base.

By waiting until this stage of the conversation and weaving qualifying questions in with impact questions, the conversation will feel more organic and not like a scripted sales call where you're trying to weed out prospects as quickly as possible.

Here's an example drawing from the ERP client referenced earlier.

How is having operational data in different databases impacting your team's ability to do their work? How many team members do you have? How many other individuals would need access to this operational data?

By weaving qualifying questions with impact questions, the prospect perceives it as a natural part of the conversation. This will help you avoid your prospect feeling like they're being interrogated.

Once you've gotten the answers to the questions and have a sense that your prospect is ready to move on, it's time to shift and describe what their world could look like with your product or service.

VP Statements

A good transition statement would be, "If it's any consolation, you're not alone. Many of our customers have experienced the same problems and challenges."

What if you could...[insert three value position statements]?

It's important to remember when using the "What if you could..." format that the questions are meant to be rhetorical. During the conversation with your prospect, don't pause at the end of delivering the VPSs. If you do, your prospect will experience something along the lines of "leading the witness."

Have you ever been in a selling conversation where the sales professional asks a question like, "If I could double your revenue in the next six months, would that be a good thing?" Or, "If I could double your revenue in the next six months, would you be ready to move forward and use our product or service?" If you phrase the problem with these types of questions, then that leaves your prospect with only one answer. Who's not going to answer yes to doubling revenue in six months. That's why they feel like they're being led and possibly manipulated. They don't have any other option in answering the question than yes.

When you're delivering the value position statements followed by a pause, it can cause the prospect to feel like they're being led. To avoid this, only pause for a second or two and then transition into a statement like, "You can, by partnering with our company."

Using the ERP example for this part of the conversation would sound like this:

"If it's any consolation, you're not alone. Many of our clients have experienced the same challenges.

What if you could:

1. Run leaner, strengthen customer loyalty, and increase your bottom line?
2. Respond to market changes while increasing efficiencies in your operations?
3. Have freedom and peace of mind to focus on your company's growth and innovation?

(Brief pause)

You can, by partnering with ERP Software Company."

Proof/Does

Once you've painted a picture of a better world by using your product or service, now it's time to explain how your product or service works and provide proof.

It's important to keep the explanation of how your product works as simple as possible. Avoid the temptation to go into a log of detail. You'll want to save the detail for the next conversation. If you provide too much detail, it may confuse your prospect, lead to more questions, and leave you without enough time to address them in this very short call.

Providing proof can happen with a brief testimonial or a one-sentence case study. In either case, you'll want the proof as relevant to your prospect as possible. Pick a client or clients from the same industry, size, and similar challenges faced.

A one-sentence case study follows this simple formula:

As a matter of fact, XYZ Company was faced with severe operational inefficiencies where now they are able to better serve their clients by using our ERP software.

Three simple elements go into the sentence. Name of a relevant client, the primary challenge they faced, and the outcome they were able to achieve. You have the opportunity to create a number of unique one-sentence case studies depending on the persona and market.

Objections/Close

I've had the opportunity to observe and question hundreds of sales professionals over the last nine years. One of the questions I am commonly asked is, "How do you transition out of a discovery call into the next stage in the sales process?" Or more specifically, "What do you say at the end of a discovery call?"

Most answer that question with a reasonable response, but some seem confused or not certain as to what they should say or ask at the end of the call. You read earlier in this chapter the importance of using open-ended questions in your conversation. Just like in the middle of the discovery call when you ask, "What does this look like in your world?", there's a similarly powerful open-ended question that you can ask at the end of a discovery call.

We've covered a good bit of ground, so what do you think?

When you ask that question, "What do you think?", it communicates respect and interest in wanting to know what the prospect is thinking. You should avoid asking yes or no questions like, "Have you heard enough in our conversation to move to the next step?" If the answer is no, where do you go from there? It's hard to recover from a yes or no question when the prospect says no. However, when you ask an open-ended question like, "What do you think?", it gives the prospect an opportunity to share with you exactly what they're thinking.

Their response will typically fall into one of three buckets.

The first response falls into the positive feedback bucket. "I love the fact that we can streamline operations," or "I love that my team can spend more time on things that are going to move our company forward." What they're doing is paraphrasing the value position statements that you communicated earlier in the conversation. When they do this, you can give yourself an A+ in your assessment of the discovery call because this is exactly what you want them to do. It has more of an impact on your prospect when they hear themselves saying the values that they recognized, as opposed to you summarizing the value at the end of the conversation.

The second bucket is clarifying questions. During the course of the conversation, you may have communicated something that they are still confused about which will cause them to ask questions so that they can better understand what you said. Keep in mind as they're asking additional questions, you have to make a decision as to whether or not you should dive deeper in answering the questions or go ahead and move toward closing for another conversation where you can go into a deeper discussion around the how, what, and where of your product. If you give too much information in this discovery call, you may not have the opportunity to go deeper later in the relationship. They may form an early impression from the discovery call that leaves them not wanting to move forward.

The third bucket would fall into the category of objections. You've already read in chapter 5 a technique called reframing that can be used to reframe emotional or biased objections. When your prospect gives an objection that starts with "I think," "I feel," or "I believe," anything that comes after that is going to be rooted in emotion or a bias. In this case you'll want to use a reframe that you've prepared for that specific objection.

If you give too much information in this discovery call, you may not have the opportunity to go deeper later in the relationship. They may form an early impression from the discovery call that leaves them not wanting to move forward.

Logical objections are pretty straightforward. Your product or service may not have a specific capability which would lead them to logically push back in the conversation. If this is the case, you'll just want to respond to the objection by showing them an alternative or a creative solution that would overcome their logical objection.

Continuing the reference to the ERP Software Company, here is an emotional objection that they get and the corresponding reframe.

Objection: "I'm a small user of QuickBooks; your price feels too high."

Response: "If I understand you correctly, based on your experience with QuickBooks, you feel like our pricing is too high? I can understand why you would feel that way. It's probably a lot like someone would feel if they were moving from a flip phone to a smartphone. The flip phone has value in that you can make calls and text. The smartphone has way more value because of all the different things you can accomplish with one device. The price difference is dramatic, but so is the functionality. That's kind of like moving from QuickBooks to our software. QuickBooks has value in its ability to manage the financial part of your business. However, our software offers more value in the same way the smart phone does. You can manage every part of your business. As a matter of fact, ABC company had the same concern. After implementing our software, though, they'd never consider going back to QuickBooks, just like you wouldn't want to go back to a flip phone. Now what do you think?"

Again, reframing an objection is not a silver bullet. In some cases, after asking the question, "Now what do you think?", you'll still hit a roadblock. But remember, this is the right technique to use when facing an emotional objection. It gives you the best opportunity to move your prospect to realizing the value of your product or service.

Once you've addressed any questions or objections, there's another great open-ended question you can ask at this point in the conversation.

"Where do we go from here?"

By asking this question, it gives your prospect the chance to share with you their thoughts about next steps in the relationship. It also gives you some insight into the decision-making process for your prospect's company. If they're somewhat vague in their response to this question, you can take the lead and suggest the next step. In most cases, the next step will involve making sure that other stakeholders in your prospect's company will be attending the next meeting. That meeting will be more focused on demonstrating how they can have the value they heard in the discovery call.

To make it easier to pull all this together and create a discovery call framework for your product or service, I've included an example bonus discovery call script. The script is broken up into five main sections that track with the sales conversation road map. The five sections are introduction, challenges and impact, value position statements, proof, and a call to action. By using this example to create your own discovery call framework, it will ensure that your prospect perceives high value around your product or service, will help you uncover pain points and needs, and give yourself a higher probability of your prospect agreeing to the next conversation.

BONUS DISCOVERY CALL SCRIPT

Introductions

Typical Leads

Use this introduction format with your usual prospects.

Our ERP software is the leading ERP software solution for thousands of companies worldwide. We offer a comprehensive, flexible, and afford-able way to manage and grow your business. The purpose of this call is to share with you at a high level how you can more efficiently grow and manage your business. At the conclusion of the call, if it makes sense, we can schedule another meeting that would allow for a deeper conversation around the information we discuss today.

Is there anything else that you'd like to cover?

(Prospect answers.)

Before we dig into this information, could you take a minute to tell me a little bit about your role at [company], about your team, goals, and some of your key projects?

Inbound Leads

If it's an inbound lead and they already have some insight about your product or service, use this introduction instead.

> *(After introductions.) Thanks for reaching out to us. Would you mind sharing what prompted you to contact us?*

(The answer that they give will provide a jumping off point into the impact questions in the Challenges and Impact section. In this case, you can skip sharing the Challenges and Impact and move right to the impact and qualification questions.)

> *Thanks for sharing. In talking with other [insert title], we hear a lot of the same dynamics holding businesses back from growing efficiently.*

Challenges & Impact

Use this script to help guide how you will address Challenges and Impact with your prospect.

> *Thanks for sharing. As we work with other [insert title], we hear that they are looking to grow their business and deliver high quality products through the use of software that provides visibility and management for their business.*

However, they're challenged with:

- *Lack of meaningful operational insights like inventory, supplier performance, purchase order workflow, and end-to-end financials.*
- *Time-consuming and complicated methods to get necessary business information out of disparate systems like QuickBooks and Excel spreadsheets or another ERP.*
- *And costly consulting fees due to lack of flexibility and difficult to use existing software.*

What that means is...

- *You and your team are wasting time chasing the information you need.*
- *There's difficulty scaling or growing the business.*
- *And, customer service may suffer due to operational inefficiencies.*

That's what we're hearing in conversations with other business leaders. I'm curious, what does this look like in your world?

(As they answer the question, you'll ask follow-up questions that allow you to deepen the impact of the challenges and qualify them as valid prospects. Questions like...)

- *What are some of the limitations of your existing software?*

- *What have you tried to solve these problems?*
- *What's the impact on your team members?*
- *How many team members use these systems?*
- *How do these problems impact your customers?*
- *What happens if you can't solve these problems?*
- *What are you using now?*
- *What is your process for selecting the right software, and who else are you talking to?*
- *Who is involved in the decision-making process?*
- *Do you have special interfaces for third-party vendors?*

Value Position Statements & Proof

Use this script to help guide how you will deliver your VPSs.

If it's any consolation, you are not alone. Our clients have realized similar challenges in addressing these problems.

What if you could...

- *Run leaner, strengthen customer loyalty, and increase your bottom line with a holistic view of your business?*
- *Respond to market changes while increasing efficiencies in your operations?*
- *Have freedom and peace of mind to focus on your company's growth and innovation?*

You can with our ERP software.

(You can expand on how ERP software works, keeping in mind the goal is to get agreement for a follow-up meeting where the details can be covered.)

Our ERP software offers one integrated business management solution for all your growing business needs, ranging from finance to manufacturing to human resources and everything in between. Our flexibility offers the most cost-effective ERP solution on the market today, with TCO up to 70% lower than comparable ERP systems. As a result, our customers benefit from on-time/on-budget projects, minimizing risks and costs.

Statement of Proof

You'll provide your prospects with a statement of proof next, like the one below.

That's how Phillips Safety was able to efficiently grow their business by moving from financial software to our ERP platform.

Closing

Here is where you'll be closing the call and addressing any objections your prospect may have. Use the script below as a guide to formulate your closing and common objection responses and reframes.

Closing Statement

> *What do you think?*

(You should hear them feed back to you the value that you communicated in the value position statements during the first call. Answer any questions and then close for the next appointment, if appropriate.)

Objection from Prospect

> *I'm a small user of QuickBooks, your price feels too high.*

Response

> *If I understand you correctly, based on your experience with QuickBooks, you feel like our pricing is too high? I can understand why you would feel that way. It's probably a lot like someone would feel if they were moving from a flip phone to a smartphone. The flip phone has value in that you can make calls and text. The smartphone has way more value because of all the different things you can accomplish with one device. The price difference is dramatic but so is the functionality.*

That's kind of like moving from QuickBooks to our software. QuickBooks has value in its ability to manage the financial part of your business. However, our software offers more value in the same way the smartphone does. You can manage every part of your business.

As a matter of fact, ABC company had the same concern. After implementing our software, though, they'd never consider going back to QuickBooks, just like you wouldn't want to go back to a flip phone.

Now what do you think?

(Prospect responds.)

Where do we go from here?

(Prospect responds.)

What most of our clients do at this point is schedule a demo where we can go into greater detail as to how our ERP software can help grow your business. Can we look at our calendars and schedule the demo?

CHAPTER 8

INCREASE VALUE IN
NEXT STAGE CONVERSATIONS

In chapter 7, you learned how to use the Sales Conversation Road Map to engage prospects in a discovery
call.

In this chapter, you will learn how to prove or demonstrate how the prospect can realize the value you communicated in the discovery call.

It's not uncommon after an initial discovery call for
your prospect to loop in other individuals that would be
involved in evaluating your product or service. When this
happens, there is a need for the other team members to be
brought up to speed on the initial conversation. One of the
more effective tools in accomplishing this is through the
use of whiteboarding.

Whiteboarding was introduced as a result of an ad
campaign that UPS ran back in 2007. UPS wanted something that would differentiate them from other shipping
companies. There's something compelling about an individual standing in front of the room and telling a story

using a visual representation like a whiteboard. During this ad campaign, more and more businesses started to see how they could use this same approach in their selling conversations.

The benefits of whiteboarding are many. The unexpectedness or unknown in the success formula is part of what makes whiteboarding work. When you're telling a story around a whiteboard, the audience has no idea of what's coming next, so it creates a sense of intrigue. This means the audience will listen more intently and pay attention and remember the main points made during the delivery of a whiteboard.

Here's an advantage that most people do not think about. When you're having a conversation with a prospect, you're trying to build credibility. When you use a PowerPoint presentation in your selling conversations, who do you think your prospect believes created that PowerPoint? The answer is typically not you. This means you're not getting full credit for what's being communicated through the use of PowerPoint. However, when you stand in front of the room or use whiteboarding in the context of Zoom, you get credit for everything that's being said because your prospect believes that the whiteboard story that you're delivering is happening in the moment.

The final benefit of whiteboarding shows up in one of the elements of our successful sales checklist, sight. John Medina in his book *Brain Rules* (2009) found that if you have a verbal conversation with someone, they'll remember about 20% of what is said two days later. If you anchor that same conversation around a simple whiteboard, they will remember over 70% of what is said. The reason behind this is that we remember things visually. When somebody says to you "remember when," you don't conjure up a ticker tape of words that were used in a conversation around that memory. What you do instead is you conjure up an image of that memory and then experience the corresponding emotions associated with the memory. Given that's the way that human beings remember, it makes perfect sense to incorporate whiteboarding in your selling conversations to make it easy for your prospects to remember what is said and, maybe even more importantly, be able to tell the story to others in the same way that you told it to them.

The sales conversation road map plays an instrumental part in creating a whiteboard story. Once you have put together a sales conversation using the sales conversation road map, you can pull up that clean sheet of 8.5 by 11-inch white paper and draw the narrative that you've created.

While doing this, there are three things to remember.

Number one, the whiteboard needs to be simple enough that a sixth grader could draw it. This means you'll be utilizing illustrations like stick figures, geometric shapes, or simple drawings like a clock or a hill. There are a couple of reasons for this. If you don't possess an artistic gift, you'll never attempt to whiteboard because it's too complex to draw. Ideally, you'd like your prospect to be able to draw and retell the story that you're telling them, and if they are not artistic and your drawings are too complicated, they won't do it. The other reason is, in the context of a selling conversation, it's important to be able to execute these whiteboard stories as quickly and confidently as possible.

Number two, the whiteboard needs to visually show the contrasting worldview that you're communicating in the sales conversation road map. You'll be drawing what your prospect world looks like today versus what their world could look like with your product or service. To create this contrast, there are several things that you can do when whiteboarding. Spatial orientation can play an important role because most people view down as bad and up as good or left as bad and right as good. This means the bad part of the story should start either on the left or lower left portion of the page. You have the opportunity to use different colors, as well. Red normally is associated with bad or negative while green and blue are typically viewed as good or positive. This means that you can use these different colors to also create contrast.

Number three, stay away from known visual frameworks. Things like "the tip of the iceberg." When you use a known framework, it robs the whiteboard of the intended intrigue you're wanting to create with your prospect. Once they see an iceberg or an umbrella or a bridge, they mentally check out a little bit because they start to realize where you're going in the drawing, diminishing the un-known aspect.

Creating whiteboards is an iterative process. It's rare that you'll sit down with your sales conversation road map story and be able to draw this visually in your first pass. The important thing is to start somewhere. Whatever you come up with initially, you can share that with colleagues, friends, or family and get their input on how to make it better. Over time, as you're whiteboarding with prospects, you'll start to see things that you can do to make the whiteboard and corresponding story clearer and more compelling.

Demonstration

Use the whiteboard to recap the initial conversation to ensure any new team members are up to speed. If it is the same individual, there is still value in walking through the whiteboard drawing to reinforce the first conversation.

You can transition from the whiteboard drawing to the demo by saying, *"Let's take a closer look at how this works."*

The demonstration is a deeper dive into what they can and can't do around the three value positions, using the demo as a proof source. You'll want to show them how you can solve the biggest challenges they identified in the first conversation.

As you explain how your product or service works, you want to briefly ask and have them describe how they are doing things today that don't work well before showing them how they can do it better with your solution. This creates the necessary contrast to communicate high value during the demo.

Find points during the demonstration after each feature to ask, "What do you think?" as well as at the end of the demo. Use these opportunities to understand where you need to clarify or overcome any objections.

Using the same ERP company example, here are the most common features you'd want to highlight and questions you would ask before showing them the feature in the ERP software.

Mobile access to information

Question: How and where do you access the information you need to run your business? How do your employees access the information? How does this impact your business?

Now show them how easy mobile access is in the software.

Business Process Management (BPM)

Question: What business processes are creating problems for your business?

Examples: enforcing price quotes, delivery time frames, team member notification, etc.

Question: What business processes are the most critical for your business? How do you manage this today?

Question: What's the impact of these things on your business?

Now show them how easy it is to simplify business process management.

Send information out of ERP Solutions to Excel

Question: How are you creating Excel reports today? How many, how much time does it take?

Show them how easy and quick it is to export to Excel.

Report generator

Question: What does it take to create custom reports today? (Expect probable answers like Excel, crystal reports, third party, or lots of time and expense.)

Show how easy it is to create custom reports.

Talk/chat

Question: How do you and your team collaborate on critical information you need to run your business? (Probable answers include creating a report and sending to team members, taking time to call them individually, etc.)

Show them how easy it is to collaborate in the software.

Realizing that not every company has software that they're demonstrating, these principles can still be utilized in a second or third conversation with your prospect. Instead of running through a software demonstration, you'll be focusing on what they can't do today as a result of not having access to your value positions. So before showing them how your value positions work, you'll want to ask them how they do it today. As they answer, make sure to ask impact questions to deepen the pain and understanding of how they are doing things today. Once they've shared this information with you, then you can transition into what they can do differently with your solution in a deeper dive into how that works.

CHAPTER 9

MASTER NEGOTIATING

Powered by The ADAPT Negotiation
Methodology
By Colby Brannan

Red Pill/Blue Pill

If you've seen the movie *The Matrix*, then you'll remember the iconic scene where the main character, Neo, is given the choice to take either the red pill or the blue pill. The red pill meant learning the potentially unsettling truth about the world, whereas the blue pill would allow him to remain in blissful ignorance and continue living his "normal" life (The Wachowskis 1999).

Like Neo, this is your moment. Do not read any further ... take the blue pill ... if you do not wish to understand the fundamental, and potentially unsettling but powerful, truth about what negotiation is and isn't. If you are ready to proceed, though, read on ... take the red pill ... but beware. What you'll see and learn throughout this chapter cannot be unseen or unlearned. You'll learn the truth about negotiation and the ironic contradictions that come with it. You'll learn about its complex simplicity, its unintuitive intuitiveness, and its linked but distinct nature when it comes to selling.

You're In?

Excellent. To begin, it's critical to understand *why* we negotiate. Why we must go through the dance of negotiation and why it's a necessary part of life and, especially, the sales process. God did an incredible thing when He created the need for negotiation. It gives us a mechanism to protect ourselves, to build value, to truly understand one another, and to be creative to find solutions. But as we know intuitively, not all negotiations are the same. There exists a multitude of situations, moments, and circumstances that give rise to the need to negotiate. Labor disputes, hostage negotiation, marriage counseling, buying a car, and so on all require forms of negotiation. In this chapter, however, I'll be focusing on commercial negotiation, where two parties are coming together to negotiate a business arrangement. Specifically, I'll be focusing on how a salesperson can be better equipped to negotiate a deal with their counterpart.

To begin the journey, however, we must be aligned on the why, so that we'll have a common frame of reference. There are four key *whys* of negotiation, and I've listed them below in order of importance. These four things are crucial—memorize them and keep them written down nearby. They will always help bring you back to center and act as your North Star as you plan for your next negotiation.

Why Negotiate?

1. To protect the business and yourself.
2. To give satisfaction and the perception of a "fair" deal.
3. To get the best possible deal for me that is acceptable to the other party.
4. To create value (when and if possible).

First, as we'll see throughout the rest of this chapter, it's important to remember that you're negotiating first and foremost to protect the business and yourself. Getting a deal closed is not the same as getting a good deal closed. In fact, closing a bad deal can create a ripple effect and unintended consequences that can be detrimental to a business over time.

For example, let's say you're trying to close a deal by the end of the year so that you can hit your quota. You decide to throw in some extra discounting and valuable options to incentivize the buyer to agree and get it over the line. The deal closes, and you make your number for the year. Congratulations! But what else has happened? For one, you've given away value that you may not have needed to give away, reducing the profitability of the deal. You've also now set a precedent with the client that anytime there's a deadline on your side, they can wait until the last minute and likely receive concessions. Lastly, and perhaps most insidious, you've potentially and unknowingly set a new and lower price ceiling that can be used against you in future negotiations. In the short term, you got your deal. In the long term, you may have unwittingly impacted the future financial health of the company.

I recently worked with a small company who sells professional services, and I asked the CFO what the average discount of a deal was for the previous year. He said, "Good question. Let me crunch some numbers, and I'll get back to you." A few days later, he calls to tell me that the average discount on deals for the previous year was 27%. Based on the tone of his voice, I could tell that this number was surprising and much higher than he had thought. I then asked him what it would mean to the business if they could reduce that discount percentage by just 5%, or even 10%. He quickly ran some more numbers and determined that a 5% decrease in discounting would yield nearly $2 million in additional revenue for this small company and close to $1.5 million more in EBIT (Earnings Before Interest and Taxes). If they could reduce discounting by 10%, it would deliver an extra $3.5 million in revenue and almost $3 million more in EBIT. For a company of this size, it was a significant amount. The salespeople at this company were excellent and very high performers. But over the years, discount-creep had set in, and the price ceiling had gotten lower and lower. In my experience in working with companies of all sizes, this is not an unusual situation. But it highlights both the insidious nature of discount-creep and the incredible impact that negotiation has on the profitability of a company.

Fundamentally, deals are reached when both sides believe it to be a "fair deal." Or, put another way, both sides are satisfied with the deal on the table. The way in which you negotiate will either generate satisfaction or it will create dissatisfaction. A skilled negotiator knows this and negotiates in a way that delivers satisfaction (or a sense of "fairness") – regardless of the actual outcome.

A comment about fairness: we can never fully know what the other party believes is a "fair" outcome. What in life is actually fair anyways? Fairness is a construct, a perception; it's not an actual thing that can be measured. Therefore, as negotiators, we need to create the perception of fairness and deliver a measure of satisfaction so that the other party can feel good about saying yes to the deal. If they do not feel the deal was "fair," or if satisfaction is not delivered, then it's likely they won't say yes or will reluctantly say yes and won't want to come back again.

Be careful with the idea of fairness. It can be very easy to give away value out of a misguided sense of it. Often, we use the concept of fairness as just an excuse to give things, thinking that by doing so we are being fair and the other person will like us more so we can conclude the deal faster. Remember when I mentioned that ironic contradictions exist in negotiation? This is one of those situations.

To illustrate this point, there's a well-known psychology experiment and game involving two people. One person has a certain amount of money and is instructed to make an offer to share any amount with the other person. The other person can only accept or reject the offer. What typically happens is that the other person will reject the deal if they believe it's not fair, even though any amount of money would be more than they had before the experiment. It's a great example of how the need for the perception of fairness can often trump logic and reason. As a skilled negotiator, it's important to keep this in mind as it's one of the driving forces behind getting to a deal.

Instead, make it your goal to get the best possible deal for you that the other party can accept. If you approach negotiations this way, you'll naturally be more protective of the business and less likely to give things away out of a sense of "fairness."

Lastly, skilled negotiators know how to create value – *when possible*. Not all negotiations are the same, and, therefore, you will not be able to create value in all situations. However, once you understand how to identify the type of negotiation you're about to enter, you'll be able to tailor an appropriate strategy.

I'll teach you a repeatable process and methodology for preparing and executing professional negotiations.

Fundamental Negotiation Truth #1:
Selling and Negotiating – Linked but Distinct

Salespeople are often terrible negotiators. I have some authority to say this because I spent nearly twenty years of my career in sales prior to becoming a negotiation expert. Looking back over the deals my colleagues, managers, and I closed, I can see now with great clarity that we left a lot of value on the table. I can also see where and at what points value "leaked" from the deal through what we *thought* were negotiations with the prospect.

There are two reasons salespeople tend not to be great negotiators. First, they treat negotiation as just an extension of the sales process. In essence, most salespeople try to sell their way through it. Selling through a negotiation feels intuitive as you continue to try to persuade your counterpart to go along with your way of thinking. But it's critical to understand a fundamental truth about selling and negotiation – they are linked, but distinct.

Think for a moment about the last time you felt you were "being sold to" by someone. How did you feel? What was your physical reaction? Did you notice a feeling of resistance start to build as the other person was clearly trying to talk you into something? These are natural responses that come as a result of feeling pressured to do something. There's a psychological theory called *reactance* to describe what is happening. "Reactance is an unpleasant motivational arousal that emerges when people experience a threat to or loss of their free behaviors"

(Steindl *et al.* 2015). Clearly, if you are trying to negotiate a great deal, you want to minimize the impact of this resistance and focus on creating the most value possible.

Second, negotiation is fundamentally different than selling. It requires different skills, behaviors, and systems. Ironically, the very skills, behaviors, and systems you have as a salesperson can work against you as a negotiator. Salespeople by nature are rapport builders. We want the prospect to like us and to see us as trusted advisors. We want to be easy to do business with and tend to say yes quickly to things so as to clear the path to the sale. We also like to talk … a lot … which directly contradicts, and can actually betray, our efforts to get the best possible deal.

Closing the Deal Doesn't Mean It Was a Good Deal

Many salespeople believe they're good at negotiating simply because they've been a high performer or have closed a lot of sales. While I certainly understand that success in sales is easily measured via quotas, I caution you against thinking that sales success equals negotiation success. You could be a top performer, yet close deals that are less than optimal for yourself or the company. We've all seen (or perhaps been) salespeople who favor quantity over quality. Quotas are hit, but at what cost to the business-client relationship?

In some ways, sales success perpetuates bad negotiation behavior. That is, unless you've been trained on how to professionally negotiate. The Dunning-Kruger effect explains this phenomenon. It's a cognitive bias whereby people with low ability at a task (or in this case, low understanding of how to professionally negotiate) overestimate their ability ("Dunning-Kruger effect" n.d.). In essence, the more we close deals and hit our quota, the more our overconfidence in our negotiating ability is bolstered. Throughout my career, I've found that most salespeople have been through extensive sales training, but very few have been through formal negotiation training. Because of this, they have no frame of reference for evaluating their true negotiating performance other than looking at their quota attainment. The assumption is, "I'm hitting my quota, therefore, I'm a good negotiator." The graph below shows the Dunning-Kruger effect as it relates to confidence levels and negotiation experience/understanding.

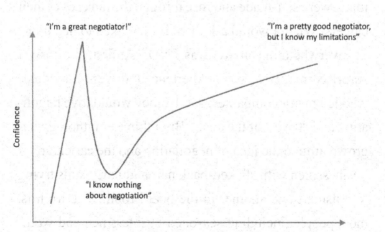

Fundamental Negotiation Truth #2:
All Negotiation is a Conflict

Perhaps the most important thing to understand about negotiation is that, by its nature, it's a conflict between two parties that needs to be resolved. Even in the most collaborative situations, negotiation represents a form of conflict whereby both sides are trying to get something that they want, which means the other party has to give something. A skilled negotiator understands this and accepts this fundamental truth, and all that comes with it.

I spent a lot of time with executive leaders of Fortune 500 organizations throughout my career. These are some of the smartest business minds and leaders in the world; many were self-made and rose through the ranks over their careers. When I would ask them if they liked to negotiate, the overwhelming answer was, "NO." At first, this answer surprised me. Here were experienced, driven individuals who led major companies; surely, they would love negotiating and "the art of the deal." But I think a mythology has grown around the idea of negotiation and the caricature of businessmen with slicked-back hair and fancy suits trying to outsmart one another in the board room. The truth is, most people, including seasoned businessmen and women, do not like the act of negotiating. It's uncomfortable, stressful, and fraught with danger.

This is especially true within the sales profession. As I noted earlier, the skills, behaviors, and systems that make a salesperson successful are often counter to the skills, behaviors, and systems that lead to successful negotiations. In some ways, you could say there are two conflicts occurring during the negotiation: The conflict that exists between buyer and seller and the internal conflict and cognitive dissonance that a salesperson deals with while negotiating.

When we sense conflict, our bodies instinctually move into a protective state, often referred to as fight or flight, or, as Daniel Kahneman refers to it in his book, *Thinking, Fast and Slow*, "System 1 thinking" (2015). When we're in this state, we tend to be highly reactionary, more emotional and governed by our amygdala. As a negotiator, this is a terrible state to be in. If you are reactionary and emotional in a negotiation, you can bet that the other party will walk away with the better deal. It's very difficult to protect the business, or yourself, if you're negotiating in this state.

You may remember the iconic photograph of Muhammed Ali standing over a knocked-out Sonny Liston. Ali was known for using a technique dubbed "rope-a-dope" whereby he would bait his opponents by pretending to be trapped against the ropes only to bounce back and taunt them over and over. Ali knew that if he could keep his opponent in a state of "System 1" thinking, while he remained consciously aware and under control, he could exploit their reactionary and emotional responses to win the bout.

As a negotiator, it's critical that you understand how to remain consciously aware of yourself and your words and actions when in conflict situations. Being aware of when you've gone into "System 1" thinking and making a conscious choice to resist being emotional and reactionary will help you take charge and remain in control of the negotiation so you can protect yourself.

Fundamental Negotiation Truth #3: Let it Be

One of the most common mistakes of the untrained negotiator is to rush through a negotiation by looking for some kind of middle ground or way to split the difference and try to conclude a deal as quickly as possible just to get it over with. This happens because, as we now know, negotiation is a form of conflict and is often uncomfortable. In an ironic contradiction, skilled negotiators *want* a level of conflict to be present in the negotiation because *it's in the resolution of that conflict where satisfaction and a sense of fairness is created.* Unfortunately, by the time you're finished reading this chapter on negotiation, I will not have removed any discomfort you feel in your negotiations. But hopefully you'll see that the butterflies you feel are an important aspect of the dance. Let the discomfort be. Embrace it and know that it's necessary to create satisfaction. What should really make you nervous is showing up to a negotiation and *not* feeling the butterflies. This is a tell-tale sign that you're either underprepared, overconfident, or you'll capitulate quickly when things get tough.

Fundamental Negotiation Truth #4:
Effort Equals Equity

The things we tend to value the most in life are the things we've had to work hard for. When we've had to work to get something, it creates a sense of ownership, pride, and satisfaction when finally obtained. Conversely, we tend not to value things highly if they've come easily to us. Understanding that people value things that they have to work for is a fundamental principal of negotiation – yet one that is counter to traditional sales behavior.

Imagine for a moment that you're in the market for a new car. You walk into the dealership, see the car you want, and begin imagining the feeling of driving off the lot in your new wheels. The sticker price of the car is $45,000, but you know very well that the price is negotiable. Imagine then that it's time to negotiate and you decide to offer $42,000 for the car. You can feel the butterflies in your stomach as you wait for the salesperson's reaction to your offer. "Great," he says, "You've got a deal!" and he reaches out to shake your hand. Now at first you may think this is a good thing, but as you go to shake his hand, a feeling of dread comes over you. This was too easy. The salesperson didn't put up any kind of fight…there was no conflict. What are you feeling at this moment? How satisfied are you with this deal? How fair do you feel that it was? Likely, even though you got the car for less than the sticker price, you're not feeling great about the deal.

Now let's imagine another scenario (the more common scenario). You go to the dealership, see the car of your dreams, make the offer of $42,000, and then wait with butterflies for the salesperson's reaction. "Whoa," he says. "That's well below the price for this car, and I've never seen us go that low on this model." The salesperson shakes his head and looks somewhat annoyed. He goes away, and after a few minutes of seemingly endless silence, the salesperson comes back and says, "Okay, I've spoken with my manager, and he said I could come down by $500. I pushed back on him because I can tell you love the car and got him to take $1,000 off." You then proceed to haggle back and forth for what feels like an agonizingly long time, finally agreeing to a price of $43,450. What would your level of satisfaction be now? You've had to work really hard to get a good deal. You paid a little more than in the first scenario. But how do you *feel*? This is the power of letting there be a level of conflict in negotiation.

Remember, it's *in the resolution* of the conflict where satisfaction and a sense of fairness is created. Even in highly collaborative negotiations, it's OK to make things just a bit difficult to get. That way, when you finally give that thing, your counterpart values it much more, and satisfaction is created. Effort equals equity.

Fundamental Negotiation Truth #5:
Get Out of Your Head

Salespeople have a lot of stresses and pressures floating around in their heads that come as part of the territory. The constant stress of meeting quotas, sales meeting performance, forecasting properly, building a pipeline, reviewing a pipeline, and so on makes the sales profession a stressful way to make a living. Of course, the personal and professional rewards are great as well, and they are the driving forces that make the pressure worth it. But the unique stresses, pressures, and desires that salespeople deal with are also the very things that can often suboptimize or even derail a negotiation.

Stress and pressure lead to emotional "System 1" decision-making. In the example I gave earlier about trying to close a deal by the end of the year in order to meet quota, there was intense time pressure and personal pressure to get the deal done. The performance-focused nature of sales adds even more pressure to an already uncomfortable negotiation. Naturally and somewhat predictably, this leads salespeople to negotiate from inside their own heads, focused on their own stresses and pressures. Without realizing it, they often enter into negotiations already in "System 1." The awareness of this tendency alone can help transform the way you approach negotiation.

In poker, they say, "You don't play the cards in front of you, you play the man across from you." And while I'm not equating negotiation with gambling, the same axiom is true. If you're stuck in your own head, thinking about your own stresses, pressures, deadlines, and rewards, you'll fail to understand your counterpart's. And unless you know those things, it becomes nearly impossible to negotiate effectively. Focusing on your own challenges limits your ability to be creative, opens you up to potential manipulation by the other party, and often leads to significant value being left on the table.

Don't become a victim of your own stresses, pressures, and desired reward. Instead, get in the head of your counterpart. What are their stresses? What timeframes are they working within? How are they compensated/bonused? What pressures are they feeling, and from whom? How is their business doing? What public commitments have been made by their leadership? Do the research, listen intently, ask great questions, and you'll start to see the big picture from the other party's perspective. Now you can negotiate from a position of knowledge, strength, and "System 2." You can make logical decisions, remain aware and conscious of your behavior, and negotiate by leveraging your understanding of their world to influence the outcome of the deal.

Fundamental Negotiation Truth #6:
Power Is Mostly Perception

Power is the unseen force that shifts the value of everything. We see this play out every day as we read about negotiations in politics, sports, business, and so on. We know intuitively that the party with more power is usually the party that has the upper hand. But, in the spirit of red pill/blue pill, if you know a little about power and where it comes from, you can leverage it when necessary or use it to protect yourself.

It's fascinating that when I'm working with salespeople and ask them who has more of the power in a negotiation, them or the buyer, they almost unanimously scream out, "The buyer!" Yet when I've worked with buyers and ask them the same question, I'll hear, "The seller!" How can this be? Both sides fervently believe that the other has more power than they do in most situations. The answer is fairly simple and has two parts. First, see my Fundamental Negotiation Truth #5. It's human nature to be stuck in our own heads when trying to make decisions. Add the conflict element of negotiation, and we tend to dig in even more. When we're

> *More often than not, it's the perception of power that carries the biggest influence.*

in our own heads, we tend to credit the other party with more power than they really have. Second, and most importantly, power is largely about perception. There are certainly situations where the power clearly lies with one side or the other due to specific circumstances (who has the negotiating power when there are multiple bids for the same item?). But more often than not, it's the perception of power that carries the biggest influence. How we behave, the things we say or don't say, the information we reveal, the use of silence, and staying in control of the process are all ways to help pull the perception of power more in your favor.

There are several levers of power, including time constraints, changing business circumstances, and alternatives or options. A strong negotiator knows to look for these levers in every situation, and also knows to be careful about sharing the first two bits of information with their counterparts unless absolutely necessary. On the other hand, sharing that you have options or alternatives can be helpful in pulling the power meter over to your side.

But be careful. With power comes responsibility. If you wield your power without regard to the type of relationship you have, or want to have, with your client, you risk damaging the relationship either now or in the future. We're seeing this play out now in these current inflationary times. Inflation (hopefully) won't last forever, business circumstances will ultimately change, and people have long memories for how they were treated when you had the power. What comes around goes around – especially in negotiation.

Fundamental Negotiation Truth #7: Not All Negotiations Are the Same

Intuitively, I think we understand that not all negotiations are the same. The situation and circumstances for each will vary and, therefore, so must your approach and behavior.

The realization that we need to proactively adapt to the situation, not just react to it, will help improve your negotiations immediately.

The two biggest determinants as to how your negotiation will go are strategy and behavior. By strategy, I'm referring to how you open your negotiation, how you make your moves, and understanding your walk away points. Behavior pertains to your demeanor, body language, verbal and non-verbal cues, and self-awareness. Strategy and behavior are equally important in ensuring the best possible outcome.

There are several types of negotiations that you could be in, but I've found that most negotiations fall into one of three types:

- Distributive
- Trading
- Value creative

There are key things to look for when determining the type of negotiation you're entering into, but the main thing to remember is *it's not necessarily what you want it to be*. It is what it is – never make assumptions. Instead, look at the facts and circumstances surrounding the negotiation, and use the checklists I've provided to determine what type of negotiation you're about to go into and, therefore, what strategy and behavioral plan is appropriate.

Remember, it's not productive to try to sell your way through a negotiation. To be a professional negotiator means that you assess the situation and adapt your strategy and behavior to that situation. Salespeople often try to justify and explain why they want what *they* want. But negotiation is not about what you need and want. *It's about what the other person is prepared to give you.* If you approach negotiations as just an extension of selling, trying to convince the other person to give you something you want, you'll likely encounter significant resistance as the other person notices you're selling and stiffens up to protect themselves.

Let's look at the different types of negotiations and the strategies and behavioral considerations for each.

Distributive Negotiations

Distributive negotiations are those in which value is distributed from one party to the other and typically centered around price as the main negotiation factor. These are your tough, high conflict, win/lose types of negotiations. We often see these when one or both sides have many options and alternatives. For example, buying a car or a trinket at a flea market often involves haggling over price. In business, we see these types of negotiations with commodities where the buyer has many similar options available in the marketplace. Or conversely, the seller has a rare or hard-to-find item and several buyers interested in the item.

With distributive negotiations, you must protect yourself at all times. There's no need for a relationship or trust because the negotiation is just a transaction. Therefore, it's critical you adapt to this and utilize the appropriate strategy and behavior to protect yourself and get the best possible deal.

These are often the most uncomfortable types of negotiations to be in because they require toughness, nerve, and behaviors that are not the norm for most people. If your natural demeanor as a salesperson is to be nice, fair, and relational, these characteristics will work directly against you in a distributive negotiation. Remember, the first reason we negotiate is to protect ourselves and the business. If you come into a distributive negotiation being nice, fair, and relational, and the other party is being tough, cagey, and uninterested in a relationship beyond this transaction, who do you think will get the better deal in this scenario?

Therefore, as uncomfortable as it may be, it's imperative that you take on certain "tough" behaviors to stay in control and protect yourself. You may need to be cold, aloof, and to the point. You'll need to resist allowing the other person's actions and behaviors to make you frustrated, angry, or emotional (System 1). You need to stay in control, in System 2, staying focused on the process. Lastly, send signals to the other person that their offers are unacceptable. By shaking your head, giving a slight laugh, pursing your lips, and so on, you send a signal that you need them to keep moving. If you don't make these gestures, they may think you're satisfied with their offer and stop conceding.

Strategy for a distributive negotiation is fairly simple. Open well higher (if selling) or lower (if buying) than what you think they will accept. This gives you room to move and, when you do start to move, builds satisfaction, so you can get to a deal. For example, if you think the most the other person will pay for the widget you're selling is $50, then open at $60 or $70. You know ahead of time that this will be unacceptable to them, but as you start to move off that number, you provide tremendous satisfaction in doing so. Try to plan your moves ahead of time – open at $60, then (after expressing a little frustration) your next offer is $54, then $51, then $49, moving in decreasing increments every time. Don't move quickly or easily; take your time, stay in charge, and show frustration with each move. By opening high and moving reluctantly, you make it difficult to get which creates satisfaction.

- Distributive Negotiation Characteristics:
  - ☐ Transactional – no need for relationship or trust between the two parties
  - ☐ Price-focused – few, if any, other variables
  - ☐ Value cannot be created
  - ☐ High conflict
- Behaviors Required:
  - ☐ Tough
  - ☐ Cold
  - ☐ Aloof
  - ☐ Firm
- Strategy:

☐ Open high
☐ Move reluctantly
☐ Plan your moves in decreasing increments
☐ Stay in System 2

Trading Negotiations

Trading negotiations sit in the middle between distributive and value creative. These negotiations require some level of trust and may include a short-term relationship after the deal is concluded. Trading, as the name implies, means that there are more variables on the table. Price is still the main focus, but there are now a few additional levers that can be pushed and pulled (traded) to impact the price.

Trading requires more trust than a transactional distributive negotiation, however, it will be important to "trust but verify." It can be easy for a salesperson to think it's OK to jump back to their natural, relational selves for this negotiation. But beware, trading negotiations can be tricky because there's still a fairly high element of conflict. Price is still the main factor, and when both sides are trying to get the best price, it will naturally create conflict.

An example of a trading negotiation could be as follows. Let's say you're selling a software package that comes with some level of support. In this case, the negotiation will need to be more than transactional because you'll be supporting the client for a period of time after the sale. So now, in addition to the price of the software package, you have support terms and perhaps payment terms and the number of seats/licenses. Price is still most important, but you can now trade the length of support, payment terms, and seats against the price.

Behaviorally, you can be a bit more open and communicate as to which levers have more impact for you and your business versus those that are less important. You'll want to understand what the other party's most important items are as well. This creates a slightly higher need for trust as you share information with each other. You also need to remember that you'll be supporting the client after the sale, so you'll need to negotiate in a way that includes *some* relational banter and attitude. But as I've mentioned above, it's critical to "trust but verify." If you over-communicate or become too relational, you could give away information that can suboptimize the deal.

Strategically, you'll still want to open high with price (higher than what you think the other party is willing to pay). But you could potentially open more reasonably with the other variables. Since you'll be levering the variables against price, you want to stay open to movement and allow for trading back and forth. For example, if the other party is willing to reduce the payment terms, you would be willing to add additional support days. Or, if the other party were to agree to your price point and payment terms, you would be willing to agree to their request for more licenses and longer support terms. As one variable moves, it will impact other variables. In these types of negotiations, you keep moving the levers until you find the combination that the other party can agree to.

- Trading Negotiation Characteristics:
    - ☐ Some relationship, some trust required between the two parties
    - ☐ Price-focused – a few variables to lever against price
    - ☐ Value is traded
    - ☐ Some conflict since price is still the main variable
- Behaviors Required:
    - ☐ Firm
    - ☐ Open
    - ☐ Sharing
    - ☐ Cautious
- Strategy:
    - ☐ Open high on some variables (generally price)
    - ☐ Trade other variables (slide back and forth) until you find the key
    - ☐ Plan your price moves in decreasing increments
    - ☐ Stay in System 2

Value Creative Negotiations

Some of the most creative and ingenious deals ever struck have come from value creative negotiations. These are typically known as win/win negotiations where both sides walk away having created value. Ironically, however, value creative negotiations are often the most complex. They require many variables, open communication, and, most importantly, very high levels of trust. As you would expect, salespeople generally enjoy these types of negotiations because there's an element of rapport building and a relational nature to them. However, as you would expect, I must caution you that even in highly relational negotiations, *it's still a negotiation*. Your job as a negotiator is still to protect yourself and the business, and to get the best possible deal that the other party can agree to. You're not there to just find the middle ground and accept the deal (a common mistake amongst salespeople).

A misconception about win/win negotiations is that both sides are splitting the value evenly. However, what really happens is that both sides feel that they've won, but one side usually "wins" a little more. Business negotiations are almost never split down the middle evenly. It's important to keep this in mind, keep negotiating, and resist the temptation to look for what you perceive to be the middle ground on an issue.

Value creative negotiations typically have many variables. In fact, the more variables at play, the more creative you can be. Variables are your levers, and the more you have, the more you can slide them back and forth to unlock and create value.

Value creative negotiations *are not about price*, they're about total value. Price is just a variable on the table, it has no higher or lower value than the other variables. It's simply one of the levers that can be used in the pursuit of total value. It's important that you resist the temptation to agree on the other variables in the deal first and wait to negotiate price at the end (a common mistake). By doing this, you risk creating a high-conflict situation, eroding trust, and potentially creating a stalemate as both sides toughen up. Instead, keep all variables on the table and available to be moved. Only when all variables are aligned do you have a deal.

Fundamental Negotiation Truth #8: Don't Give Without Getting

Consider making trades conditional. For example, "If you can do this for me, then I can do this for you." By trading this way, you're allowing a bit of tension to exist and using the psychological power of giving to get. As I mentioned earlier, if you simply give things to the other party, they won't value it. If you make them work a bit for it, even if it's just making the trade conditional, you'll find that you build much higher levels of satisfaction and even trust.

So, how do you create value? There's a simple formula for ensuring that every trade you make is creating value. As you're preparing for a negotiation, look at all the potential variables that could be on the table. Then, identify which of the variables are relatively low cost for you to give, but of high value to the other party and vice versa. Your low-cost items are your gives and their gets. Their low-cost items, which are of high value to you, are your gets and their gives. Because value creative negotiations are highly relational and require high trust, you should be able to have pre-meetings before your negotiations to sit with your counterpart and ask questions around what variables are most important to them while sharing which are important to you. When both sides understand where the value is, you can work together to unlock it in the negotiation. This does not mean that you get to the negotiation and just give your low-cost variables to them (and vice versa). It's still a negotiation. So you'll plan your moves accordingly, move with slight reluctance to help create satisfaction, move in decreasing increments, and stay in System 2 thinking, consciously aware of your verbal and non-verbal cues at all times.

- Value Creative Negotiation Characteristics:
  - ☐ Long-term relationship, high levels of trust required between the two parties
  - ☐ Value-focused – many variables (the more the better)
  - ☐ Value is created with each trade by looking for low cost/high value trades
  - ☐ Some conflict since win/win is not actually 50/50
- Behaviors Required:
  - ☐ Collaborative
  - ☐ Open

- ☐ Creative
- ☐ Flexible
- ▪ Strategy:
  - ☐ Trade low cost/high value variables to create value
  - ☐ Price is not overly important – it's just a variable used in the creation of total value
  - ☐ Plan your price moves in decreasing increments
  - ☐ Stay in System 2

Fundamental Negotiation Truth #9: Salespeople Often Negotiate in Reverse

Not only do many salespeople not enjoy negotiating, they also tend to negotiate in reverse. Negotiating in reverse is when we look to conclude a deal that is right above our own walk away point. This means, while you may have negotiated a successful deal, you've actually negotiated for the lowest available value. For example, if your walk away point for the widget you're selling is $50, meaning you will under no circumstances sell the item for less than $50, and you end up agreeing to a deal that is close to the $50, then you have *minimized* the value of that deal. Conversely, if you surmise that the buyer's walk away point for the widget (the most they would possibly pay) is $70, and you conclude the deal closer to their number, then you've come close to *maximizing* the value of that deal.

To avoid negotiating in reverse, you first need to try to determine what you think the other party's walk away point is. You'll never actually know the number, but if you get out of your own head, look at their circumstances, options, and time pressures, you'll be able to take an educated guess as to the most they'd be willing to pay. Remember, this is a *walk away point*. It's not what you think is a reasonable outcome or what you think they will accept. It's the point at which they will walk away from the deal. Once you've determined their walk away point, you can then plan your moves in a way that allows you to get closer to their number, versus landing somewhere near your own walk away point. Open your negotiation higher than their walk away point with the understanding that you will come off that number and eventually get under it. By doing this, you allow for constructive conflict to exist and create satisfaction when you finally move under their walk away.

Fundamental Negotiation Truth #10: Preparation Is Power

There's an old axiom in negotiation that 90% of a negotiation's outcome will come down to how well you prepare. And it's absolutely true. I will also say that 90% of people don't prepare. The single best thing you can do as a negotiator is to take the time to methodically prepare.

Knowing your (and your team's) tendencies, getting in the head of the other party, planning your moves, staying consciously in System 2 thinking, and so on, will ensure that you're in the best possible position to protect yourself and maximize the outcome of the deal.

Below, I've provided the ADAPT Negotiation Methodology, a process that you can follow to prepare for, and conduct, negotiations in a systematic way.

Trust The Process:
The ADAPT Negotiation Methodology

- Assess
- Determine
- Align
- Position
- Take Charge

By now, you've seen that many of the natural behaviors of salespeople are often contradictory to the behaviors of successful negotiators. It's critical that we can adapt – adapt our behavior and methods to match the type of negotiation that we're about to go into. The ADAPT Negotiation Methodology gives you a road map and repeatable process you can follow so that you avoid "System 1" thinking, stay in control, and put yourself in the best possible position for a successful negotiation, no matter the situation.

Assess (Me, Them, and Us)

"To know thyself is the beginning of wisdom." – Socrates

As we've established, negotiation is a conflict. Therefore, it's critical that we understand how our minds and bodies react in conflict. Do you have a tendency toward fight or flight? In our workshops, we'll record live one-on-one negotiations and replay them to the participants so they can see how they physically and verbally react. It's often quite surprising to the individuals because they aren't yet aware of how they unconsciously react in conflict situations.

Here are some questions to ask yourself. There's no judgement here, just a self-understanding of how you tend to react when under stress.

1. How competitive are you? (scale of 1-10, where 10 is ultra-competitive)
2. What's more important to you, fairness or winning?
3. If someone confronts you, is your tendency to bow-up/push back? Or to go quiet/recoil?
4. In conflict, are you directive/assertive or more passive/peacemaker?
5. In an emergency, do you tend to react emotionally or become focused?

Once you've identified your natural tendencies when you're under stress, you become consciously aware of how you may behave in a negotiation. Remember, the first reason we negotiate is to protect ourselves and the business. If you become reactionary and emotional when under stress, you're vulnerable to manipulation by the other party, and to suboptimizing the deal. Similarly, if you go into a negotiation wanting to win at all costs, you risk damaging the relationship (if one exists) or, again, being exploited by the other party if they're aware of your need to win. They may make you feel as though you're winning by saying things and acting a certain way because they know that winning is more important to you than the deal itself.

- ASSESS (ME) Checklist:
    - ☐ What is my natural conflict style and tendency?
        - aggressive, want to win, push back during conflict
        - fair, accommodating, look for compromise, dislike conflict
    - ☐ What are my time constraints?
    - ☐ How much do I need them?
    - ☐ What public commitments have been made by my leadership?

After honest self-reflection and determining your natural conflict style, you should then move to understand the party you're negotiating with or against. What do you think their style is? How have they reacted before? Is their natural demeanor passive or aggressive? Listen during casual banter—do they talk about competition, sports, or winning? Or do they talk about things like fairness, kindness, getting along? These clues will help you understand how they might react when the negotiation is underway and they start feeling stress. A skilled negotiator can then use this information to influence the proceedings and protect themselves.

Key Point: We negotiate with people, not businesses!

- ASSESS (THEM) Checklist:
  - ☐ Get out of your head – get in THEIR head
    - What are their pressures and stresses?
    - What are their motivations, concerns, worries, alternatives?
  - ☐ Personal and business time factors
    - When does the deal need to be done by?
    - What happens if they don't meet a deadline?
    - Do they receive any kind of bonus (or penalty)?
    - What are the financial ramifications of a delay?
  - ☐ Personal and business circumstances
    - How's their company doing compared to the market?
    - What public commitments have their leadership made?
    - What is their competition doing?
    - Are they trying to be promoted or maintain status (could indicate urgency)?

**Based on this information, what is the *real* state of POWER between us?

Lastly, if you're in a team negotiation, be sure to understand the individual and collective tendencies of your team. Nothing can derail a negotiation faster than a team that is not in sync in terms of behavior. If you have a mix of fair-minded and competitive individuals on the team, you must be aware of how these personalities will be amplified when under stress. This can cause conflict and result in mixed messaging and disunity. Everyone must self-assess and become conscious of their tendencies, and team leaders must be hyper aware of the collective behavior of the team to ensure a unified front.

Determine

Remember Fundamental Negotiation Truth #7: not all negotiations are the same. After assessing your and your counterpart's natural behavior and conflict styles, you then need to look at the situation and circumstances around the negotiation to determine what type of negotiation you're in. If we approach all negotiations in the same way, using our natural behaviors and slipping into "System 1" thinking, we are likely to be exploited by the other party and/or suboptimize the deal.

- DETERMINE Checklist:
  - ☐ What type of negotiation is this?
    - Distributive
    - Trading

- Value Creative
- [ ] What will be my behavioral approach based on the negotiation type?
  - Tough, cold, firm, aloof?
  - Firm but open?
  - Collaborative and creative?
- [ ] What are the variables at play?
- [ ] Which variables are more important to me, and which are more important to them?

**Remember your conflict style and stay aware!

Align

The Align step is where you'll start to formulate the specifics of your strategy. Fundamental Negotiation Truth #9 warns against negotiating in reverse, and this step will help ensure you're approaching the negotiation with the mindset of capturing the most value possible. First, you need to understand your guardrails, i.e., your walk away points. It's important to know at what point it's simply not worth doing the deal. This is partly how you'll protect yourself in a negotiation. Once you determine your walk away point, *set it aside and don't focus on it.* Remember that focusing on your own walk away point usually leads to suboptimizing the deal. Next, get out of your head and into the other party's head to try and figure out what their walk away points might be. What stresses and pressures do they have? What time constraints? What other options do they have? By looking at these things you can formulate an educated guess as to what their walk away points are. Finally, plan your moves *before* you get into the heat of battle. Play out the negotiation in your mind. Remember to open higher than their walk away point and then move in decreasing increments. Try to conclude the negotiation as close to their walk away point as possible – this is how you maximize the deal.

If you're negotiating as a team, ensure that you're all aligned on the walk away points, opening and moves.

- ALIGN Checklist:
    - ☐ What are my walk away points?
    - ☐ What do I think THEIR walk away points are?
    - ☐ Where will I open?
        - Remember to open higher than their walk away points (where possible) to leave room to move and create satisfaction.
    - ☐ Plan moves
        - Plan your moves ahead of time – before the negotiation
        - Goal is to land on or near THEIR walk away points
        - Move in decreasing increments
    - ☐ When trading:
        - Never give anything away without getting something of equal or greater value in return
        - "If you can do this…then I can do that."

Position

One of best ways to influence the outcome of a negotiation is to start positioning early. By positioning, I'm referring to the subtle hints and comments that you make in the days and weeks leading up to the negotiation. Positioning is not selling; it's a proactive way of managing the other party's expectations. For example, in the days leading up to a negotiation, I might express to my counterpart that I don't have a lot of flexibility on price or payment terms, but I do have flexibility on contract length and support. I'm not negotiating yet, but I've given a clue to the other party as to where my flexibility lies. Another way to position your product or service is to refer to it in certain ways during your discussions. An example would be to call your service "premium" or "on the premium end of the spectrum" (if it is). This helps set the expectation for the buyer that they can expect better quality, service, and a higher price point. Or you could position the value of support early by saying, "I'm sure there will be a lot of focus on the support aspect of this deal, given its importance." The idea is to frame the negotiation around the variables that you want to focus on. This is the opposite of reactive and helps keep you in control of the proceedings. It's also important to continue positioning during and throughout the negotiation. The way you act, the things you say, and the way you move will all have a positioning impact on the negotiation and will affect the outcome.

I'm Ron Burgundy?

A common challenge I've seen when consulting or teaching is that when people are under pressure and they've gone into System 1 thinking, they tend to use soft language when making proposals. Soft language emerges in several ways, and if you're listening for it, you'll hear it. You must guard against using soft language, but always, always be listening for it as it could indicate that your counterpart is not fully confident in their proposal. Some examples of soft language are, "We'd really like to be in the ballpark of...," or "I can do $45,000?" (voice raises as though asking a question), or "I could probably do something like..." Listen for qualifying words or words that end in -ly, like actually, really, or probably. We often use soft language when we're under stress because it makes us feel as though we're protecting ourselves. But to a trained negotiator, soft language indicates a lack of commitment and, therefore, flexibility in the offer. Once flexibility is signaled, strong negotiators will continue to push for a better deal. Instead, state your offers with firm conviction. "The price is $45,000," followed by silence while the other party reacts. This is much firmer than, "I'd like to be around $45,000." Conversely, listen closely to the way your counterparts phrase their proposals. If you hear soft language, it's likely that they're movable from their position, and you should continue to negotiate.

- POSITION Checklist:

  *Position before and throughout the negotiation – always PROACTIVE and never reactive

  ☐ Position based on negotiation type

  ☐ Preconditioning for the outcome
    - Where are you flexible?
    - Where are you inflexible?
    - Timing (their issue)

  ☐ Tone and behavior

  ☐ Satisfaction and signals
    - Make things difficult to get (even if it's easy to give)
    - Silence
    - NO SOFT LANGUAGE
      ◊ Don't pad your words: "I'd *really* like to be in the ballpark of" or "in the *range* of X"
      ◊ Eliminate *actually, probably, basically, honestly*

  ☐ Negotiating, not selling
    - Don't try to convince them via persuasion or solely on facts and figures
    - Don't get in an argument – will only create an emotional response

Take Charge

The final element, and the key to ensuring a successful negotiation (after you've prepared, of course) is to take charge of the proceedings. Take charge of the timing and cadence of the negotiation. Get your variables and positions on the table before they do, if possible. Manage your behavior and tell them what needs to occur. Fundamental Negotiation Truth #1 states that selling and negotiating are linked but distinct. To take charge of a negotiation means you stop asking for what you want, and instead, *tell* the other party what needs to happen to get the deal done. I'm not implying that you become a jerk (that is unless you're in a distributive negotiation, in which case you might need to in order to protect yourself), but you can be directive in a negotiation and remain pleasant. If you ask, "Would you accept a price of $1,000,000?" What would the answer likely be? NO! It is, after all, a negotiation. Instead, tell them "If you can align to a 3-year term, then I can align to a price of $1,000,000." In this instance, you'll still be pleasant, yet directive.

You will be uncomfortable. But remember, effort equals equity. If you allow there to be some conflict and make the other party work for what they want, they will value it all the more and perceive the deal to be fair. Don't end a negotiation early because you're uncomfortable. Realize that the other party is uncomfortable as well and *let it be.*

- TAKE CHARGE Checklist:
    - ☐ You are in control.
    - ☐ Do not become reactive to the other party's behavior, time pressures, or power plays.

☐ Anticipate their moves, behaviors, and tactics.

☐ Plan for discomfort.

☐ Remain self-aware (body language, tone, fidgeting, soft language).

☐ Be in control of time and cadence.

Final Thoughts

You've swallowed the red pill. You now understand the fundamentals of professional negotiation, with its complex simplicity, its unintuitive intuitiveness, and its linked but distinct nature as it relates to selling. You know the different types of negotiation and the strategies and behaviors that will help you succeed. You understand the importance of preparation, and you have the ADAPT process to guide you through. You should now be able to approach any negotiation with *confidence*, knowing that you can remain in control no matter the circumstance. But as Morpheus says in *The Matrix*, "…sooner or later you're going to realize just as I did that there's a difference between knowing the path and walking the path" (The Wachowskis 1999). You can do this. Protect yourself and the business. Create satisfaction and a perception of fairness. Get the best possible deal that the other party can accept. And finally, create value if at all possible.

CONCLUSION

Congratulations, you made it to the end of the book! You've read a lot and may be wondering, "where do I go from here?" Before answering that question, a quick recap. You've learned a good deal about the science of decision, how to use this understanding in selling conversations, and how to handle negotiations. It's a lot to start applying to your daily selling activities, so if you don't take anything else away from this book, pay attention to these four things:

1. Your intent in a selling relationship is key. If you'll make the primary goal serving another business professional by improving their life as a result of using your product, you'll realize success on two different levels. One, you can know you're making a difference in the world. Two, you'll put yourself in the best position to thrive as a sales professional.

2. It's up to you to communicate value, from the prospect's point of view, in every selling conversation.

In order to accomplish this, you'll need to have a deep understanding of the prospect's world. This leads to a place of empathy and gives you a better path to painting a contrasting worldview. One without you contrasted with one with you.

3. Be creative. You owe it to your prospects to stand out in the way you communicate with them during the buyer's journey. The sales profession can be one of the most creative if you'll take the time to slow down, use some of the techniques from this book, and practice.

4. Remember to understand the difference between selling and negotiation conversations. Sell first, and then negotiate when the time is right.

The process of writing this book has reminded me of my son's experience with basketball. He started playing at six years old, about a year later than most of his friends. Needless to say, he was behind the other kids in understanding the rules of basketball. The very first game it seemed like the referee had it in for him. For the first quarter and a half, the ref kept blowing his whistle, "no, son, you're going the wrong way," "nope, that's the wrong end of the court," "you can't carry the ball."

As a result of this, in the middle of the second quarter, he plopped himself down on the court and started to cry. He quickly found me up in the stands, crawled off the court up into the stands and stood in front of me and said, "daddy, I quit." I looked at him and I said, "no, son, you're not going to quit; you're going to play the entire season. All your friends down on the court have played a whole year and are able to enjoy the game without thinking about it. So, you're going to play for at least one season and if we get to the end of the season and you'd like to quit, you can." So, he played an entire season and at the end, he decided to continue to play.

Fast forward four years later and my son is playing in a competitive league in suburban Atlanta. They're in the championship game and he's the starting point guard. They end up winning the championship and at the end of the game, after celebrating with his team, he finds me up in the stands which brings a flashback to four years previous. As he was standing in front of me, I asked him if he remembered a similar scene four years ago. I said, "do you remember standing in front of me crying, saying you wanted to quit?" He answered, "yes." I looked at him and I asked if it was worth the time and effort to get to this point? He got a big smile on his face and said, "yes."

That's kind of like where you are after having experienced the content of this book. Each of us when we learn something new walk through four quadrants of learning. The first quadrant is unconsciously incompetent. In other words, you don't know what you don't know. Not to say that you've not heard or read about some of the things that you experienced in this book, but not in quite the same way that you read in the book. At some point while you're reading the book, though, you move from unconsciously incompetent to consciously incompetent. This means you start to have an understanding of what you need to do, but may feel like you're not competent to actually do it. From there is the third quadrant, consciously competent. This quadrant is where you are conscious of what needs to be done and you're competent in being able to do it. However, if you just stay in this quadrant, you'll spend more time thinking about executing a technique and not paying attention to the prospect. That's why moving to the fourth and final quadrant, unconsciously competent, is the final step in the learning journey – not just for sales, but for anything. This is where you're not even thinking about the techniques that you're utilizing; instead, it's just a part of who you are in the way that you're communicating with prospects.

Just as my son had to experience the pain and challenge of having a whistle blown at him when he was executing incorrectly, as you move through these four quadrants, you'll experience some of the same bumps in the road. However, it's worth every bump and every challenge so that you can better serve your prospects, communicate the highest value, and stand out as being unique and creative in your role as a sales professional.

If you'd like more help or assistance in applying these principles and techniques in your role, visit us at www.mastermessaging.com. In addition to blogs and other resources, you'll find an online course where I walk sales professionals through each of the steps in the book in more detail and with specific exercises that will get them to a place of excellence in the application of these principles and techniques.

BIBLIOGRAPHY

"Dunning-Kruger effect." n.d. Wikipedia. Accessed June 29, 2022. https://en.wikipedia.org/wiki/Dunning%E2%80%93Kruger_effect.

Gartner. n.d. "New B2B Buying Journey & Its Implications for Sales." Accessed April 12, 2022. https://www.gartner.com/en/sales/insights/b2b-buying-journey.

Grant, Adam. 2014. *Give and Take: Why Helping Others Drives Our Success.* New York: Penguin Books.

Hassan, Uri. 2016. "This is Your Brain on Communication." Filmed February 2016 at TED2016. Video, 14:51. https://www.ted.com/talks/uri_hasson_this_is_your_brain_on_communication.

Heath, Chip & Dan Heath. 2007. *Made to Stick: Why Some Ideas Survive and Others Die.* New York: Random House.

"Honesty/Ethics in Professions." Accessed June 14, 2022. Gallup. https://news.gallup.com/poll/1654/honesty-ethics-professions.aspx.

Kahneman, Daniel. 2015. *Thinking, Fast and Slow.* New York: Penguin Press Non-fiction.

Kosoglow, Mark. 2022. "The Best Email Subject Lines for Sales [2022 Update]." Outreach. Accessed April 14, 2022. https://www.outreach.io/blog/best-outbound-sales-development-cold-email-subject-lines-2022.

"LinkedIn." n.d. Wikipedia. Accessed June 29, 2022. https://en.wikipedia.org/wiki/LinkedIn.

McDougall, Christopher. 2011. *Born to Run: A Hidden Tribe, Superathletes, and the Greatest Race the World Has Never Seen.* New York: Alfred A. Knopf.

Medina, John. 2009. *Brain Rules: 12 Principles for Surviving and Thriving At Work, Home, and School.* Fall Rivers, MA: Pear Press.

Merriam-Webster. n.d. "road map 2." Accessed April 14, 2022. https://www.merriam-webster.com/dictionary/road%20map.

Pink, Daniel. 2011. *Drive: The Surprising Truth About What Motivates Us.* New York: Riverhead Books.

Power of Words, "The Power of Words," uploaded February 23, 2010, YouTube video, 1:47, https://www.youtube.com/watch?v=Hzgzim5m7oU.

Purves, D., GJ Augustine, D. Fitzpatrick, *et al.* 2001. "The Interplay of Emotion and Reason." *Neuroscience*, 2nd Edition. https://www.ncbi.nlm.nih.gov/books/NBK10822/.

"Salesperson." Accessed June 14, 2022. Cambridge Dictionary. https://dictionary.cambridge.org/us/dictionary/english/salesperson.

Saturday Night Live, "Verizon 4G LTE - SNL," aired February 11, 2012, uploaded August 12, 2013, YouTube video, 2:03, https://www.youtube.com/watch?v=aUYZSopmtCk.

Sinek, Simon. 2011. *Start with Why: How Great Leaders Inspire Everyone to Take Action.* New York: Portfolio.

Steindl, Christina, Eva Jonas, Sandra Sittenthaler, Eva Traut-Mattausch, and Jeff Greenberg. 2015. "Understanding Psychological Reactance: New Developments and Findings." *Zeitschrift fur Psychologie* 223(4): 205-214. https://doi.org/10.1027/2151-2604/a000222.

The Wachowskis, dir. *The Matrix.* 1999; Burbank, CA: Warner Bros. 136 minutes.

IF YOU ENJOYED THIS BOOK, WILL YOU HELP ME SPREAD THE WORD?

There are several ways you can help me get the word out about the message of this book…

- Post a 5-Star review on Amazon.
- Write about the book on your Facebook, Twitter, Instagram, LinkedIn – any social media you regularly use!
- If you blog, consider referencing the book, or publishing an excerpt from the book with a link back to my website. You have my permission to do this as long as you provide proper credit and backlinks.
- Recommend the book to friends – word-of-mouth is still the most effective form of advertising.
- Purchase additional copies to give away as gifts.

The best way to connect is by visiting
www.MasterMessaging.com

READY TO TEST THE INFORMATION YOU JUST LEARNED?

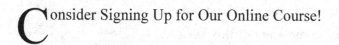

Consider Signing Up for Our Online Course!

If you'd like to learn how to apply the principles in this book to building high-value sales conversations, scan the QR code above or type in the link below to your web browser:

https://onlinecourses.mastermessaging.com